To ED:

From your FRIENDS AT
THE Santa Barbara Marit
Museum

30 May 2002

Copyright © 2002 by Devereux Books

Published by Devereux Books
PO Box 503
Marblehead, MA 01945

Internet address: www.devereuxbooks.com

Library of Congress Cataloging in Publication Data

Hunn, Peter, 1953-
Beautiful outboards / Peter Hunn.
p. cm.
ISBN 1-928862-04-7
1. Outboard motors.   I. Title.
VM341 .H85 2002
623.8'7234--dc21   2001047686

Book design by Alyssa Morris

Printed in Singapore

Contents

Getting Things Humming — **SUBMERGED ELECTRIC** 6

The "Original" Outboard Motor — **WATERMAN'S EARLY MODELS** 9

An Ice Cream Special That Runs — **EVINRUDE'S ROWBOAT MOTOR** 13

The Second Chance Gang — **LATER WATERMAN MODELS** 16

Will The Real Waterman Please Stand Up! — **SWEET** 20

Exotic Copycats — **JOYMOTOR, RACINE, AND WILCOX-MCKIM** 22

The Motor with a Few Fans — **AEROTHRUST** 26

It Ain't Heavy, It's My Koban — **KOBAN** 29

Outboarding's Big Tip — **FEDERAL** 32

Good Brand, Bad Motor — **EVINRUDE 4-CYCLE** 34

Vive La Difference! — **AMPHION** 37

Imported Iron — **KNIGHT** 39

Two Pulls Will Convince You — **CAILLE ROWBOAT MOTOR WITH REWIND** 41

Longing for Change — **CAILLE LIBERTY** 44

Setting a Standard for Speed and Performance — **ELTO SPEEDSTER & QUAD** 47

Beautiful Red Head — **CAILLE MULTIFLEX** 52

Money Isn't the Object, Speed Is — **OMC SPEEDI-BEE & ELTO #632**...................54

One of the Brothers' Best — **JOHNSON K-65**...58

Cute as the Dickens! — **CLARKE TROLLER** 61

The Other 3-In-1 — **THOR PYRAMID 3** 64

Kiekhaefer's Pollywog — **THOR STREAMLINER**..66

Milwaukee's Best Toy Outboards — **EVINRUDE MATE & ELTO CUB** 68

Ole's 'Ol Grandad of the Race Course — **EVINRUDE/ELTO 4-60** 71

Uncle Sam's Revamp — **EVINRUDE BIG FOUR** 74

The Red Head's Orphan — **RED TOP** 77

For Those Who Prefer Catching Fish On All Four-Cylinders — **EVINRUDE ZEPHYR**..........79

A Genuine Bargain — **ELGIN** 82

Classic Sea Horse Green — **JOHNSON TD** 84

Old Time Outboard Racing's Fountain of Youth — **HUBBELL** 86

Putting Stock in Outboard Racing — **MERCURY LIGHTNING, HURRICANE, AND MARTIN "60" HI-SPEED** 88

Kids and Water Skis and a Sea Horse 25 — **JOHNSON RD** 93

An Oddball Trying to Crack a Conventional Market — **FLAMBEAU** 97

The "Corvette" Outboard — **MARTIN "200"** 100

Fast Should've Lasted — **CHRIS-CRAFT RACER** 103

Today's Most Powerful Outboard! — **MERCURY MARK 50**....................................106

Slightly Understated Performance, Very Exaggerated Name — **MERCURY SILENT SIX** 109

"Look, Your Lipstick Matches Our Motor!" — **JOHNSON JAVELIN**..........................111

"Can I Get That in Sarasota Blue or Sunset Orange?" — **MERCURY MARK 25** 114

Wagging the Dog — **WIZARD 25 AND MERCURY MARK 30H** 116

The Brand X File Motor — **CONTINENTAL SPORT** 120

Too Foreign, Too Soon — **ZÜNDAPP** 123

Theory Yes, Practice No — **OUTBOARD JET** 125

"Kids Just Love 'Em!" — **MERCURY 60J** 127

Acknowledgments

At the sound of most any cellar stair creak, my memory can call up the image of freshly built, long wooden motor stands neatly arranged along three sides of Bob and Patrica Zipps's basement. There, on a crisp 1967 Saturday, I first saw a real collection of vintage outboards and was inspired to shift my youthful fascination with power boating into a full-fledged hobby focused on learning about the history of such machines and the people who manufactured them. Consequently, this book and my friendship with Bob and Pat are indelibly entwined. A subsequent association with other members of the Antique Outboard Motor Club augmented my resolve to research the outboard industry. It also provided a level pathway towards both the old motors and vital information required to make these pages possible. For the pictorial subjects of this edition, I am most grateful to Art DeKalb, Bob Grubb, and Bob Skinner. Each fellow's outboards are identified in their engines' respective specification tables. Without the cooperation of these premier collectors, *Beautiful Outboards* could not have been efficiently assembled. They were selected not only for their museum-quality inventory, but also for a brand of patience vital to a project with sundry venues, hard deadlines, and lots of lifting. Appreciated, too, is the quiet skill of our photographers; Dan Reaume for the Canadian shoot, Bill Hazzard who snapped the shutters in Pennsylvania, and Dave Dayger photographing in Central New York. Not far from the latter sessions is the Antique Boat Museum in the Thousand Islands community of Clayton. The author is thankful for the kindness and archival expertise of Antique Boat Museum librarian Phoebe Tritton. Without her help, securing original literature for this volume would have been difficult.

Finally, I would like to dedicate *Beautiful Outboards* to the memory of my sister Martha. She never complained when helping me move old motors, and once, near the top of the cellar stairs, miraculously stabilized a hefty four-cylinder Johnson V-45 headed my way after I missed a step and fell to the concrete floor. When one loses a sibling in youth, a favorite childhood snapshot image often remains. In mine, Martha, on a brightly varnished slalom water-ski is smiling between the white wake of our aluminum Lone Star runabout and 30-horsepower Johnson Javelin. Sometimes she'd shoot so far out of the wake that I could see her reflection in the chrome side wing accents of the old Johnson. If this book brings you a pleasant memory or two of enjoyable times on the water, everyone involved in its production will thankfully consider our time well spent.

The Photographers:

Dan Reaume: 6-14, 16-18 (top), 20-23, 26, 28-30, 32-33, 39, 44-46, 52-55, 61-63, 77, 78 (upper), 103-104, 106, 107 (upper), 109, 111-112, 123.

Bill Hazard: 24-25, 34, 36, 37, 41, 42 (top), 47, 50, 64, 66, 68, 69 (upper), 70-73, 100-101, 116-117, 119-121, 126-127.

Dave Dayger: 48, 56, 57, 58-59, 60 (lower), 79-80, 84, 93-94, 114.

Brochure photography by Stan Grayson.

Other photos/drawings from author's collection.

Introduction

Kids sometimes get fixated on what might seem like ordinary stuff, and I had pestered my grandmother for an ordinary adjustable wrench. The proprietor of our local hardware store matter-of-factly pointed to a cheap, rough, sand-cast tool he'd pulled from a bin and dropped onto the counter. Grammy began counting change from her purse when the shopkeeper politely asked if he could show me something absolutely beautiful. With the pride and care of a museum curator, the fellow cradled a sleek adjustable in his outstretched palms. "This is from a high-class foundry out in California," he beamed. "Light as a feather and strong as an ox. Even the trademark on its box is a work of art!" The enthusiastic display and description of provenance of what most would mundanely consider a utilitarian item were captivating. I still own that wrench, and have long associated it with my introduction to the phrase *beauty is in the eye of the beholder.*

No doubt, to the uninitiated, a book called *Beautiful Outboards* might seem like a marine oxymoron. That's because, for many of its formative years (1900-1930s), the outboard motor was a much maligned Cinderella to inboard engine stepsisters. Not until the post-World War Two family boating boom did the "sputtery old kicker" get transformed into a recognizable princess of the waterways. During the 1950s, though, and with what seemed to be overnight stardom, it went from being the cantankerous province of mechanically oriented, impecunious, salty-tongued anglers to a turnkey convenience eagerly embraced by men and women throughout the socioeconomic spectrum. Now amidst all of today's powerful, sleekly shrouded, and expensive outboard products, more than sufficient distance has been marked from the vintage one-lung, chain store putt-putts so as to be able to place the outboard industry's first century into perspective. What emerges are rows of machines that many an antique boating buff or industrial design devotee clearly view as beautiful. Hence this volume's unashamed title.

The book was created to pictorially highlight the spirit of outboard motor innovations from the early 1900s through about 1960. When one considers that this relatively brief epoch spanned from the sunset of horse-drawn travel to the dawn of the space age, the engines in this study may be seen to mirror such progress. Also remarkable is the fact that more than a few of the motors herein still see regular summer duty. Although a late 1940s Mercury 10-horse, for example, might generate a little lakeside curiosity, its performance is consistent with modern outboards. That's a testament to those who built them, and to the owners who've lovingly preserved them.

A majority of the brands represented in these pages are long gone. The early 21st Century auction of Outboard Marine Corporation assets demonstrated that even the venerable Evinrude and Johnson names were not exempt from business's winds of change. Happily, however, the reader may relax in the retrospective peace that such a photo-history uniquely affords. You'll find nicely preserved Waterman vertical-cylinder models, the quintessential Evinrude rowboat motor, an ultra-rare OMC SpeediBee racer, classic Mercs, and dozens of serendipitous oddballs seemingly designed to make one exclaim, "Wow! That's really clever!"

Admittedly, it was difficult to make the book's final motor selection. Doubtless, there are literally hundreds of engines worthy of inclusion, but the same elements of time and space that regularly confound boat and outboard collectors, played havoc with our finite table of contents. Those featured in this volume represent the preservation spectrum from arguably "better than showroom" to notably nice "as found" condition. Not all of the motors in the following pages emanated from what might be dubbed "top shelf" companies. This was planned with the understanding that those who appreciate old iron are seldom too prejudiced to miss the beauty in a Plain Jane kicker like the bargain-priced Continental Sport. My hope is that *Beautiful Outboards* both satisfies and whets the appetite.

Peter Hunn
Fulton, New York
January 2002

SUBMERGED ELECTRIC

Brand Name: Submerged Electric
Model: "Fresh Water"
Serial Number: 19
Year of Manufacture: 1900
Manufacturer: Submerged Electric Motor Company
Place of Manufacture: Menomonie, Wisconsin
Type: Electric
Weight: 30 lbs. (Battery weight, per box: 45 lbs. no. of batteries suggested: 2-5.)
Original Price: Approximately $100. Each box of batteries: $25.
Owner: Robert Skinner

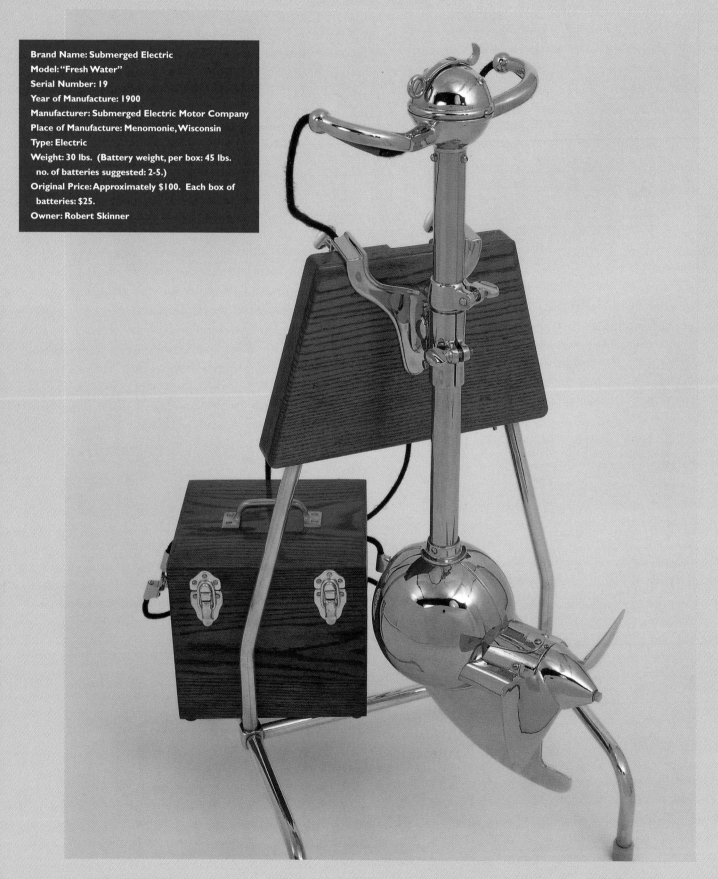

America's first super highway, the Erie Canal, spawned an ode to outboard power. Almost every late 19th Century boater who enjoyed carrying a tune knew the one about an old mule Sal that pulled her owner's craft 15 miles a day along that legendary waterway. By then though, even the most conservative small boat skippers knew that the towpath's days were numbered. Also quietly rejected was steam. It had made a little toehold in small inboard-powered boating circles, but never offered enough portability to be a viable candidate for the coming wave of widely affordable, practical outboard propulsion. As 1900 dawned, that ticket was split between gas and electric motors. In outboarding's early days, neither had a significant speed advantage over the other, and both required some sort of battery (or "accumulator"). Given equally good juice, the electric version was the more certain runner. In that milieu the Submerged Electric Boat Propeller entered the marketplace.

During May, 1899, inventor Tracy B. Hatch sought a patent for his "propelling mechanism for boats." The application noted that his "object [was] to provide an electric motor to be supported entirely or partially beneath the surface of the [water] and of a novel construction that prevents undue heating of the motor or of the resistance coil, if employed and dispenses with the necessity of a stuffing box for the motor shaft." Most importantly, he predicted the resulting device would be "compact, durable, and well adapted for its purpose" of easily attaching to, then driving rowboats and other small craft. The Chicago man was awarded a patent a year later and lost little time in assigning it to the Submerged Electric Motor Company of Menomonie, Wisconsin.

Chronologically, Hatch wasn't the originator of the electric outboard motor. That honor belongs to a W.S. Salisbury who, in 1892, received a patent for a "Boat Propelling Device" resembling an electric motor at the head end of a crooked oar, with a prop — driven through a flexible shaft — at the other. This basic contraption showed up in advertising three years later under the brand name, Allen Portable Electric Propeller. While a neat 35-pound package, the Allen required batteries that could add nearly ten times that weight. The pioneer Allen kicker appears to have been offered through 1899, coincidentally when Hatch filed

In 1900, officials at Submerged electric had few direct competitors. Still, they wanted people to know exactly when their unique portable boat-propelling device was granted a patent.

papers for his electric that, unlike, the Salisbury or Allen, operated coolly underwater. A hole in each half of the fresh water models' power ball allows water to enter and surround the motor's armature, brushes and other components normally natural enemies of liquid.

Production of the 1900 Submerged Electrics coincided with the Pan American Exposition where the Wisconsin firm distributed a souvenir booklet about the "only electric motor in the world that will operate submerged; the water having access to all its moving parts." Nowhere in the document is the term outboard motor used, as it had not yet been coined. But, the fact that the Submerged Electric "occupies the place of the rudder and can be placed in position on any boat or exchanged from one to another in five minutes," earned prominent editorial space. Inclusion of transom clamp thumbscrews — as on modern outboards — made this pledge realistic. Company officials also wanted boaters to understand that their product wouldn't blow up, make noise, get dirty, or even smell funny. Also a McKinley-era selling point was the fact that "no government inspection [was] required [of the motor, nor would there be need for the Submerged to be operated by a] licensed engineer." In fact, compared to a tiny splash of circa-1900 gasoline-fired outboards then in the curious hands of a few mechanically minded buffs, the Submerged Electric was a snap to operate.

Its primary limitation came from nascent battery technology. By today's standards, these powerpacks were ludicrously heavy and quickly drained. The aforementioned brochure admitted their rechargeable battery boxes weighed in at about 50 pounds apiece and noted some applications called for a half-dozen boxes.

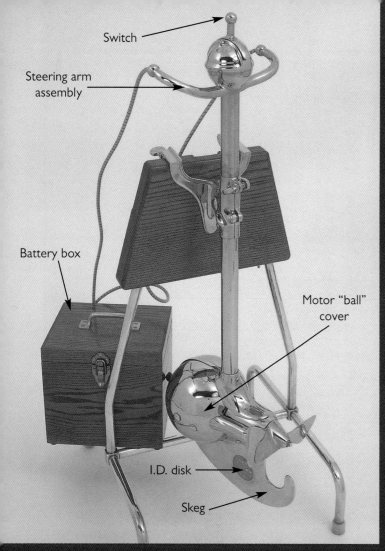

Switch

Steering arm
assembly

Battery box

Motor "ball"
cover

I.D. disk

Skeg

Originally nickeled, this 1901 Submerged received gold plating some 90 years later to make it a sparkling companion to the collector's standard silver units.

A voyage of 25 miles was promised between charges. Top speeds were said to be in the four to six mile per hour range.

The Submerged Electric Motor Company committed to offer variety. Three sizes of the ball-covered motor were promoted in the premier catalog, a 30 pounder for 12- to 16-foot boats, one weighing two pounds more for pushing craft from 16 to 18 feet long, and a 60 pounder rated to handle up to 22 footers. Salt-water versions were offered in each model. They differed from the regular Submerged in that "the outer case of the motor is so constructed that it can be filled with [a quart of] fresh water to cool the electric powerplant] through an opening in the tubular stem."

Our 1900 Submerged subject motor enjoyed a complete rewind some 99 years after leaving the factory. Well over 200 hours of restoration and case polishing gave this electric a performance and sheen at least equaling its baby picture in the Exposition booklet. The gold plated 1901 model is what one might call "retro-mod," in that the owner decided to go the orig-

inal nickel plate one better and treated it to a 24 karat golden layer for a stunning effect. Finally, the 1902 model had a series-wired parallel switch enabling the operator to tap into six batteries for fast spurts of about five-plus miles per hour, which rivaled most any of its gasoline-fired contemporaries.

Continual gas engine technology advances along with the fledgling battery industry's failure to discover ways to improve the power-to-weight ratio stymied the Submerged Electric Motor Company's ability to gain or sustain market share. In 1906, the concern advertised a gas outboard engine, but it's unclear whether or not any were built. Three years later, the firm left the outboard field. It is possible the Submerged Electric may be linked to a subsequent New York City product. There, in 1931, an obscure company called, Mayfair Boats, introduced a submerged electric motor for small boats. Dubbed, Silver Streak Electric Drive, it notably resembled the motor in Hatch's patent. None of those Depression-era products are known to exist. Meanwhile, the Submerged Electrics pictured here represent some of the world's oldest outboard motors. Each can still hum right along.

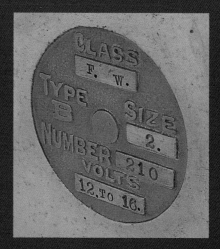

"F.W." referred to this 1902 Submerged model's fresh water-only status. Holes in the "powerhead ball" allowed cooling water to circulate through the motor's electrical parts such as it armature. "S.W.," or salt-water versions had a water jacket around the "powerhead ball" to be filled with tap water. The surrounding seawater would in turn, keep this fresh water cool. S.W. owners were told to change the fresh water periodically.

WATERMAN VERTICAL CYLINDER MODELS

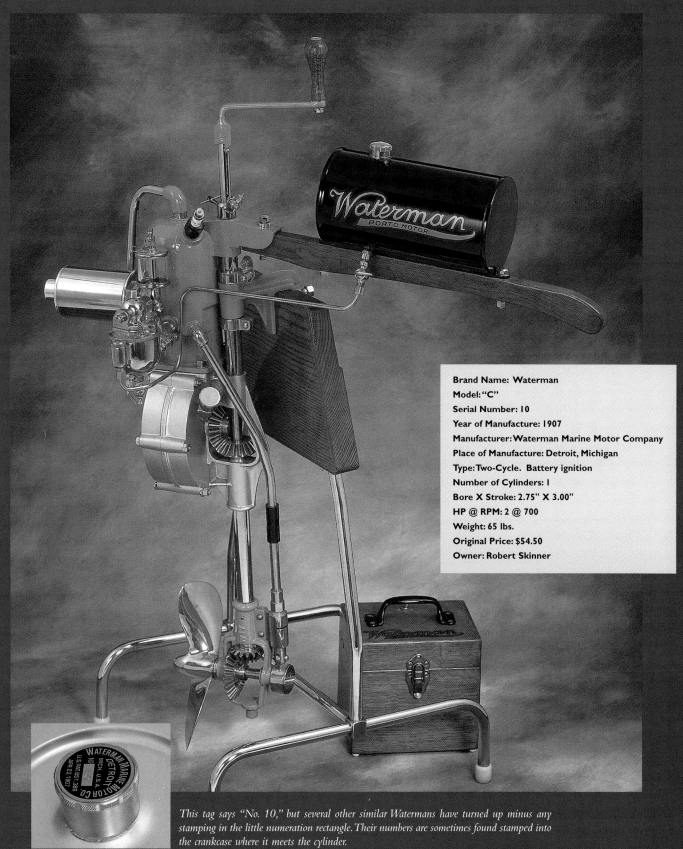

Brand Name: Waterman
Model: "C"
Serial Number: 10
Year of Manufacture: 1907
Manufacturer: Waterman Marine Motor Company
Place of Manufacture: Detroit, Michigan
Type: Two-Cycle. Battery ignition
Number of Cylinders: 1
Bore X Stroke: 2.75" X 3.00"
HP @ RPM: 2 @ 700
Weight: 65 lbs.
Original Price: $54.50
Owner: Robert Skinner

This tag says "No. 10," but several other similar Watermans have turned up minus any stamping in the little numeration rectangle. Their numbers are sometimes found stamped into the crankcase where it meets the cylinder.

It's unlikely that, during his college days, Cameron Beach Waterman had a chance to come across a Submerged Electric Boat Propeller. The native Michigander spent the first several years of the 20th Century busily studying law at Yale. He did have time, though, to participate in the University's crew team and do some motorcycling around the Connecticut campus. Late one chilly fall, when the motorcycle season was curtailed by snow, Waterman used the hiatus to remove the bike's engine and take it up to his dormitory room for a cleaning. Clamped to the back of his desk chair, the little motor's new perch reminded Waterman of a small boat's stern. Suddenly, the tedium of rowing popped into his mind, and the idea of an easily mounted, lightweight boat motor crystallized in response. The concept followed him back to Detroit after graduation. By 1905, he and a local industrialist friend began working on a prototype of what Waterman was first to dub an outboard motor. Actually, a fishing buddy came up with the descriptive nomenclature, but was happy to have it adopted for Waterman's new venture. This version used a stock, single-cylinder Curtiss motorcycle powerplant and chain drive — soon replaced by a driveshaft — to the propeller. With the invention judged as worthy of even further refinement, engineer Oliver Barthel was hired. His influences got the outboard ready for commercial production in late 1905.

When, decades later, Barthel and Waterman remembered this era, exact dates and initial model year offer-

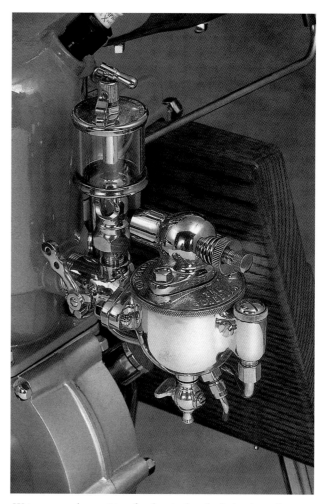

Waterman used a variety of carburetor brands during its early years. Waterman literature from the 1906-1909 period indicated the motors would be shipped "with the best available carburetion. This small Schebler was one of the best.

Resting on the Waterman ignition's dry-cell battery box, is the lower unit's clamp. Because most rowboats of the pre-1910 era typically had stern posts rather than flat "outboard motor-type" transoms, this clamp could be affixed near the post's bottom, allowing a round protrusion at the base of the Waterman lower unit to be held and swiveled there.

ings appeared a bit hazy. It seems, however, that 25 air-cooled Waterman motors were built in 1906. Some — reportedly from this batch — had external flywheels, which shot spray all over the place upon frequently hitting the water's surface. This was corrected by enclosing the flywheel inside the crankcase, as the one on the Curtiss mill had been harbored. The water-cooled design most associated with surviving examples of the early Watermans was said to have been developed after the summer of 1906. A run of 3,000 of these outboards was counted as 1907 model year production, but the first group to be assembled was probably sold in 1906. Keeping meticulous manufacturing date records often took a back seat to more exciting developmental endeavors. It is also now duly noted that Waterman production numbers probably included its popular inboard engines such as the single-cylinder model K-1. Exact model/year deliniations were con-

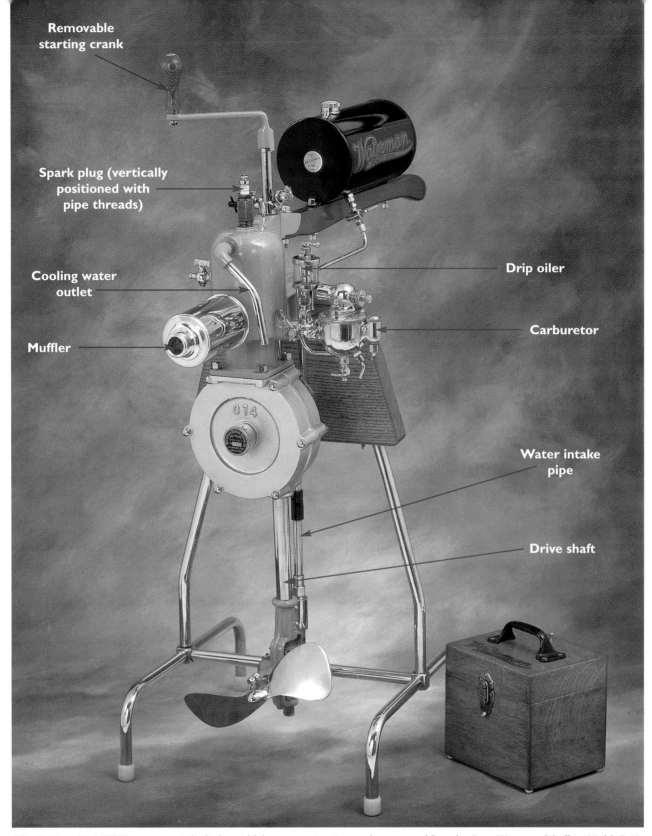

Removable starting crank

Spark plug (vertically positioned with pipe threads)

Cooling water outlet

Muffler

Drip oiler

Carburetor

Water intake pipe

Drive shaft

The C-14 on this 1909 Waterman vertical cylinder model denotes a part casting number, not a model number. Later, Waterman did offer a Model C-14. Updated from the company's first commercial design, this generation Waterman can be most easily distinguished by the vertical — as opposed to slightly tilted — pipe thread spark plug. During assembly, pistons were hand-fitted into the cylinders. Consequently, restorers trying to make one good motor from two derelicts often find that the piston, from one 1909 Waterman, for example, won't quite fit the cylinder of another. Note: The brass button on the fuel tank end is the restorer's trademark.

veniently ad hoc. As a result, collectors trying to zero in on specifics are often forced to be satisfied with a 1906-1907 designation. Most distinguishing of this generation is the tilted spark plug, as opposed to vertical plug placement in 1908 through 1910 engines.

The Waterman Model "C" on page 9 wears an early enough serial number to be honored with a 1906 birth date. Even so, to be on the safe side of the previously mentioned tenuous record, it is identified in our specification box as a 1907. That seniority in the outboard world prompted its restorer to devote nearly 325 hours to the revitalization project. Truthfully, Waterman model "C," serial number 10 looks better today than it ever did in 1906. Waterman tillers, for example, didn't receive the fine degree of sanding and varnishing as the one shown here. Pictures of these motors built well before World War One suggest that they couldn't rival the appearance of our subject motor. Dented fuel tanks, faded and scratched decals, as well as evidence of overall rigging were the almost immediate provinces of this pioneer lot.

In a 1950 retrospective, Cameron Waterman was certain that each of his fledgling company's 3,000 outboards built in 1906 and another 3,000 the following year, quickly found buyers. Again, though, those numbers were likely tainted with inboard production figures. At that late juncture in Waterman's recollections, it's understandable that all of his factory's motors were simply remembered as "motors made." He credited the 1909 sale of 6,000 Waterman kickers to the fact that Evinrude had just begun operation, causing the boating public to take the idea of outboard motoring more seriously. Actually, little production occurred at Evinrude until 1910. Once it did, though, Evinrude would start eclipsing Waterman's enviable position as

Propeller blade   Propeller   Water pump   Water intake
                   drive gear

Waterman owners were advised to keep the lower units well greased. With an exposed system, such a mandate could be frustrating to obey. Note water pump in front of gear frame. The little horizontal slit served as intake.

the primary name in outboarding. Indeed, Cameron Waterman's company had offered the world's first successful, widely advertised and distributed outboard motor. Anyone coming across Evinrude's better design, however, was likely to go with that newcomer. The Evinrude rowboat motor looked more self-contained and user-friendly than the gangly Waterman with its vertical cylinder, exposed gearing, and precariously removable crank starting handle. Waterman tried improving the original motor — even to the degree of adding a faux, top-mounted flywheel for 1910 engines — but it didn't require Waterman's Yale education to understand that a completely different model was now needed in this suddenly competitive industry.

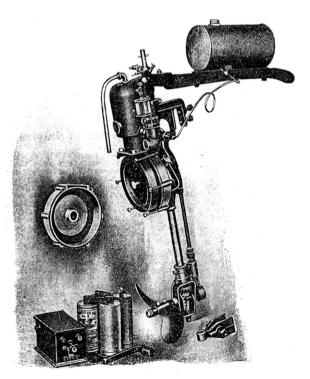

1908 catalog depiction of Waterman outboard with flywheel cover removed. Ignition accessories are also shown.

An Ice Cream Special That Runs

EVINRUDE'S ROWBOAT MOTOR

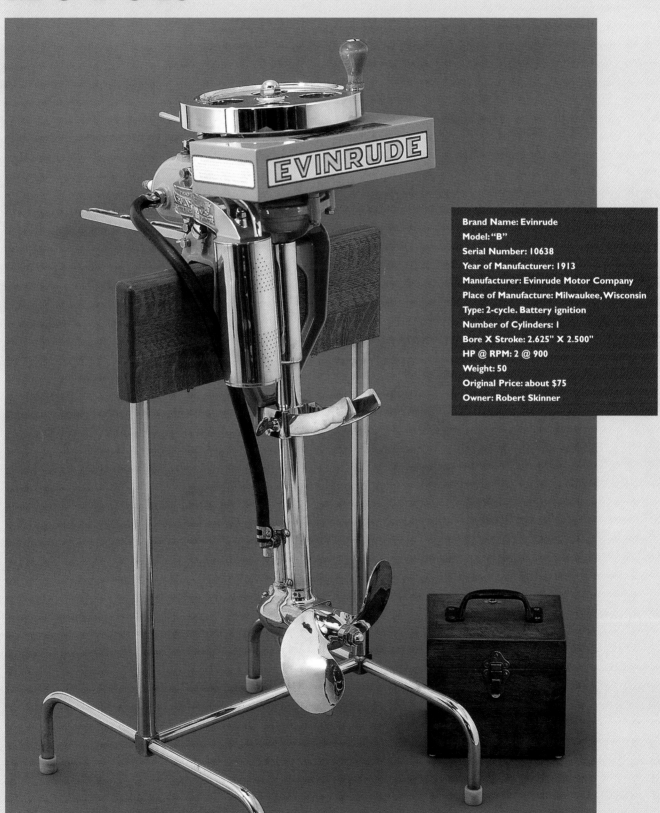

Brand Name: Evinrude
Model: "B"
Serial Number: 10638
Year of Manufacturer: 1913
Manufacturer: Evinrude Motor Company
Place of Manufacture: Milwaukee, Wisconsin
Type: 2-cycle. Battery ignition
Number of Cylinders: 1
Bore X Stroke: 2.625" X 2.500"
HP @ RPM: 2 @ 900
Weight: 50
Original Price: about $75
Owner: Robert Skinner

I n 1949, personal and confidential correspondence from the maker of Mercury outboards arrived at the Waterman household. The letter, written by Merc CEO, E. Carl Kiekhaefer, asked Cameron Waterman to play an important role in debunking an increasingly popular Evinrude story — a romantically endearing tale that was said to explain the Evinrude brand's pioneer status.

This piece of pleasure boating apocrypha surrounded a loving couple, ice cream, warm summer sunshine, a picturesque lake, and rowing. No one is quite sure where the story originated, but in a 1947 promotional booklet, *Ole Evinrude and the Old Fellows,* Gordon MacQuarrie promulgates that the Evinrude "family history thoroughly and accurately records" it. It is an account of Ole Evinrude, his fiancée, Bess Cary, and a group of friends picnicking on an unidentified island in an unidentified Milwaukee area lake. Reportedly, Bess asked Ole to get her some ice cream. He rowed two miles to a store, bought the treat, and then rowed "facing a growing wind" another two miles back to the island. Naturally, the ice cream quickly melted. During the frustrating voyage, Ole is credited with a eureka moment in which the notion of an outboard motor materialized. The tale ends happily with Ole marrying Bess, followed by his invention of an outboard motor that made the couple rich and famous.

Prior to 1911, most Evinrude rowboat motors were void of the elaborate exhaust casting trademark. The company also produced pumps driven by a similar outboard powerhead. On these engines, some of the exhaust castings had the boat but no motor astern.

Apparently, no one checked those aforementioned accurate family records before shifting the event's occurrence from 1907 to 1906, recalling that it was definitely on Lake Okauchee, stating that the ice cream had been in cones, forgetting the other picnickers, and moving the distance from two, to three, then, as a 1952 *New York Herald Tribune* noted, "a tortuous five-mile row." Besides, Bess was nobody's fool and would never have expected ice cream to stay frozen while competing against the scorching August sun. No matter the literal veracity, however, it was an American epic few outboard buyers could resist.

There's little doubt that Ole Evinrude had seen other outboard motors before building one around early 1909. In fact, a 1922 catalog indicates Ole had worked with a man who developed an outboard. Arguably, this was Harry Miller, the racing car engine designer, who, years earlier, employed Evinrude. Photos still exist of a gas-fired kicker with an underwater powerhead that Miller prototyped before concentrating on Indianapolis Speedway cars. There's reason to believe Ole had at least heard of this curious contraption. And with some 6,000 Watermans in use by 1909, it's also quite possible that tech-hungry Ole might have spied one running or otherwise been a recipient of hearsay about the innovative mechanical device.

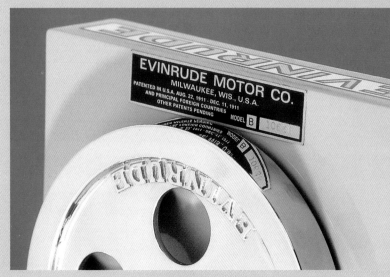

This rare shot of an Evinrude rowboat motor pulled immediately from the production line may be compared to the one in our color photograph. Restored engines sometimes look prettier than new originals! The squeeze lever on the tiller activates a tilt-lock mechanism.

Classic public relations department scenario aside, Ole's first outboard was judged by Bess to look like a "coffee grinder." She suggested he dress it up a bit. Ole translated that as tremendous encouragement and improved the powerhead innards along with the exterior's rough edges. Bess articulated her approval when a fellow who had borrowed this motor returned to their doorstep with several paid orders for more. Ole hadn't even considered pricing, so he told the customer that $62 sounded OK because the outboard weighed about that number in pounds. Her head for business complementing Ole's mechanical expertise, Bess established an Evinrude Motor Company office. The new partner's first contribution was a simple, but effective ad commanding, "Don't Row! Throw Away The Oars! Use An Evinrude Motor!" This upbeat message contrasted with oddly apologetic drumming for rival Waterman's outboard, "Don't Be Afraid Of It!"

Clearly, the early Evinrude rowboat motor represented revolutionary design integration. A forward pointing single cylinder, rear fuel tank, and flywheel starter knob bested Waterman's vertical jug, tiller-mounted tank, and precarious crank. The Envirude made the Waterman look like a "contraption." While almost no subsequent competitors followed the vintage Waterman layout, nearly every newcomer, through about 1920, copied Evinrude basics. Some of this plagiarism was due to Ole's naïve habit of offering engineering advice to anyone who dropped by the factory. Visitors included Messers Harley and Davidson of motorcycle renown. They needed help with a troublesome carburetor, and toyed with the idea of marketing a Harley-Davidson outboard a lot like Ole's.

By 1913, the date our featured Evinrude single left the factory, the company had sold over 10,000 outboard motors around the globe. That year, Ole added a half-horsepower to his original one-and-a-half horse 1909-1912 model. Also new for '13 was the skeg cast below the lower unit gearcase. It was meant to protect the propeller and aid in steering. Chances are that our subject motor passed by Ole as he checked the assembly line. Then again, by late 1913, his thoughts were largely focused on Bess. She had been taken ill and was seldom in the plant anymore. Without her there, Ole decided to sell the company. He even agreed to sign a letter blocking him from participating in the outboard industry for the foreseeable future.

Boat power wasn't only thing the Evinrude factory endeavored. Here, one of its rowboat motor powerheads is installed in a walk-behind garden tractor. Several companies bought the engines for a variety of uses.

The Second Chance Gang

WATERMAN'S LATER MODELS

Brand Name: Waterman
Model: C-12
Serial Number: 105
Year of Manufacture: 1911
Manufacturer: Waterman Motor Company
Place of Manufacture: Detroit, Michigan
Type: Two-cycle, Three-port, Water-cooled
Number of Cylinders: 1
Bore X Stroke: 2.750" X 3.0"
HP @ RPM: 2 @ 850
Weight: 64 lbs.
Original Price: $65
Owner: Robert Skinner

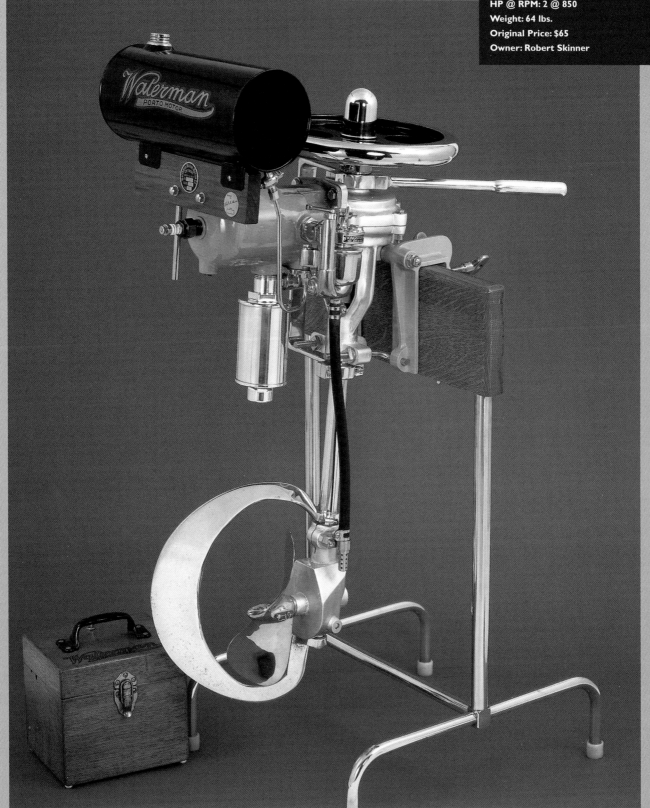

W aterman catalogs were famous for divulging emotion between the lines. C.B. Waterman had hoped to trademark the term outboard motor, but registry bureaucrats found it to be too generic and descriptive. Disappointed, he dubbed his outboard products "Porto" — short for portable — then peppered sales brochures with subtle zingers broadly aimed at anyone who dared to enter the fledgling business that bore the description he pioneered. "As was to be expected," 1913 Waterman literature mused, "other manufacturers attempted to build detachable marine motors. Some of them changed the design to avoid our patent, while others tried to build engines cheaply. Within a year or a few months, one [outboard firm] after another gave it up, and our old reliable Porto kept on making new friends and keeping the old friends, too."

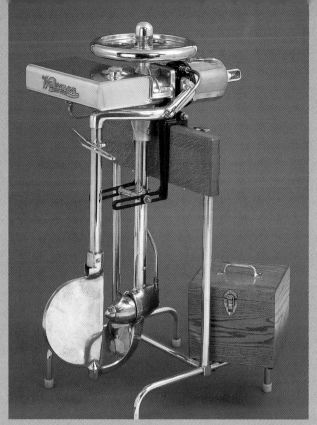

By 1914, when this model C-14 was offered, Waterman had begun using rectangular, instead of tubular, fuel tanks. For quick and accurate oil/gas measurement, one could pull off the little flywheel cap and fill it with oil sufficient for a tank full of gasoline. The rudder support served as underwater exhaust outlet. Some clothesline could be tied to the steering bracket for control anywhere aboard. The metal sparkplug "protector" not only kept a bumped plug porcelain from cracking, but kept voltage away from careless hands.

Interestingly, most notable of the leading pioneer makers who had given up the ghost in time for a dubious eulogy in Waterman's 1913 document were the likes of a short-lived trio; Burtray, Water Sprite, and Walnut. Each brand had mimicked the palsied-performing, vertical cylinder design of the original Waterman Porto. Almost exclusively, the Detroit firm's true challengers discounted the vertical format in favor of a horizontally placed cylinder made famous by Evinrude. Not that Ole's motor was historically the first with such configuration — the 1896 American often gets that esoteric honor. But, through evidence of sheer sales volume, the pleasure boating public quickly accepted Evinrude as early outboarding's most sensible package. Understandably threatened, Waterman sent his engineers looking for ways in which a new "Porto" could be part of this undeniable design trend . . . without looking too much like an Evinrude.

Referring back to 1913 Waterman catalogs, one ascertains that the "original outboard motor" company, as its admen touted, "had designed a horizontal engine in 1907," two or three years prior to Ole's ice

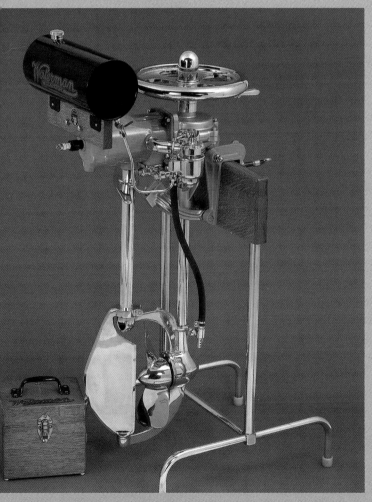

The term "giving the motor a spin," could be applied to this C-13 Waterman from 1912. By gripping the flywheel, then quickly rotating it, that's how one started the motor. Note rudder design change from earlier 1912 (C-12) model.

After buying the Waterman interests, Arrow Motor and Machine Company eventually began selling Watermans under its own name. This one is on an Arrow Waterman model C-16 clone.

cream revelation. Unfortunately, though, it was "not as perfect as [Waterman] had wished." With hyperbolic candor, the jealous firm indicated that "during 1911, the last slight defects (which would not have been considered by less careful manufacturers) were overcome and [Waterman] began to advertise and sell [the] Model C-12.

Although meant to be released as a 1912 motor, C-12 #105 shown here is thought to be a product of fall 1911. Company records indicate the entire C-12 production run had been shipped by July 1912, so an improved version, the C-13, went on sale during the remainder of 1912 and most probably through the following winter. Aside from the rear-pointing, horizontal cylinder, enclosed lower unit gears, and crescent-shaped rudder, the C-12 (and its slightly younger C-13 sister) is remembered for its unique two-in-one focus. That is to say, Waterman advertised that owners could easily take this Porto off a rowboat, loosen a few bolts and set screw, remove the lower unit, bolt the powerhead to a small

base, then have a stationary engine for running a saw, pump, or other outdoorsy accessory. Of course, these endeavors required a nearby water source for keeping C-12 or C-13 cool.

Arguably, the heated pace associated with Waterman's ad-hoc midseason model changes was caused by regular Evinrude advances and the growing number of clones hitting the market. Even the Caille Perfection Motor Company, in whose Detroit tool room the first Waterman castings were poured, began producing a line of outboards. Perhaps because Waterman had already made the big step from vertical to horizontal cylinder positioning, the flip from rear pointing to an early Evinrude-esque forward-facing cylinder was not so hard. Labeled the C-14, this Waterman became available during 1913. Outboard buffs consider this model to be the quintessential Waterman. In fact, within most vintage powerboating circles, the C-14 is the Holy Grail of the industry's seminal period. The C-14's combinations of spun copper, aluminum, cast iron, bronze, and bright plating, yielded beautiful results. The Antique Outboard Motor Club, Incorporated has long seen fit to feature this engine in its official logo.

No doubt, that would have pleased Cameron Waterman. But, by the mid-teens, most outboard buyers didn't seem to appreciate Waterman's pioneering efforts anymore. They demonstrated this by buying an

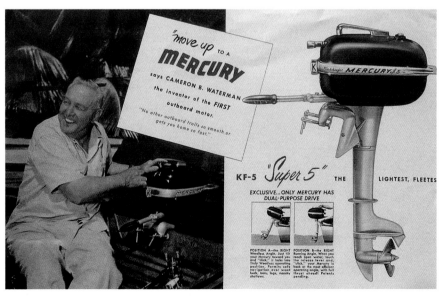

Here is Cameron Waterman as shown in Mercury's 1950 catalog. Mercury chief E. Carl Kiehaefer also honored Waterman at numerous boat shows and sporting writer's luncheons as a means of weakening Evinrude's "first in outboarding" claims.

increasing number of Evinrudes, Cailles, and other latecomers' motors. That's not to say the Waterman marque had no devotees. Just enough boaters bought Waterman engines — inboard as well as outboard — to keep the founder revamping the Porto (into the model C-16 with oversize flywheel and variable pitch propeller) and warning consumers about his competitors. "We feel it our duty," he noted in a 1916 prospectus, "to advise against being influenced by the catalog talk about some [other maker's] engine where one or two special features overshadow every other detail." But by then, Evinrude outboards weren't even being made by Waterman's old competitors Ole and Bess. They'd sold the shop to an investor and were leisurely enjoying an indefinite sightseeing phase.

Meantime, the outboard industry had billowed to a point where a rush of firms oscillated in and out of business like dot.com companies would do some 85 years later. It's quite likely that in this roller coaster milieu, Waterman reminded himself that, after all, he was really supposed to be an attorney, and didn't need aggravation caused by fickle consumers easily swayed by outboards highlighted in some Johnny-come-lately's

brochure. In 1917, Cameron Beach Waterman agreed to sell his company to a minor New Jersey rival, and then delved into law while the entire industry he'd founded simply passed him by. Some three decades down the road, there'd be one notable exception. In the pages of yet another outboard company's catalog, Mr. Waterman would get a new introduction.

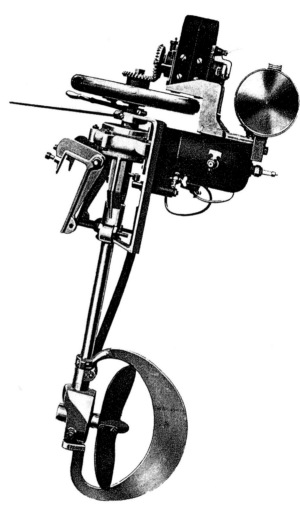

1911 Waterman C-12 with accessory magneto

Waterman **PORTO** Motor

Makes a Motorboat of Any Boat in Five Minutes.
1914 MODEL THE RESULT OF 9 YEARS EXPERIENCE.

THIS illustration shows something of the beauty of the "Waterman"—but don't you buy any motor by the looks alone. The all-important thing to get is certainty that the motor will give lasting satisfaction, and the only way to be sure of this is to bank on the experience of others, and the reputation and standing of the factory behind the motor. Let "the other fellow" experiment with the untried imitations. Keep your money until you know what you are buying.

3 H.P.
Weight 59 Lbs.

Most Power
for the Price.
Most Power
for the Weight.

The Waterman "Porto" is the original outboard motor. It is guaranteed for life. Nine years successful use—25,000 delighted "Waterman" owners and every one a "Waterman" booster. The "Waterman" fits any shaped stern (attached or removed in a jiffy) and drives a rowboat, dinghy, tender or other small boat eight to ten miles an hour, thirty miles on a gallon of fuel.

Buy Direct from Factory
Freight Prepaid Anywhere in the United States.

Don't buy an outboard motor of any make until you get our free engine book and learn the "Waterman" terms and price, and find out about the superior features of the "Waterman." You will be sorry if you fail to insist upon these features in the motor you buy:

Carburetor, not "mixing valve;" 3 Piston Rings instead of 1; Removable Bronze Bearings; 10½" x 16" Propeller; Independent Rudder; 25 feet of tiller line, steers from any part of the boat; Noiseless Under-Water Exhaust; Bronze Gear Pump, forming Valveless Water Circulation System; Spun Copper Water Jacket, highly polished; Ignition: Bosch, or any other strictly high grade high tension magneto; or by battery. DEMAND THESE FEATURES IN ANY OUTBOARD MOTOR YOU BUY—OR YOU ARE NOT GETTING THE WORTH OF YOUR MONEY.

Immediate delivery assured, either direct from Factory or from nearest distributor's stock. Keep the Agent's Profit.

Postal brings free engine book and full information.

Waterman Marine Motor Co.
401 Mt. Elliott Ave.
DETROIT, MICH.

Will the Real Waterman Please Stand Up!

SWEET

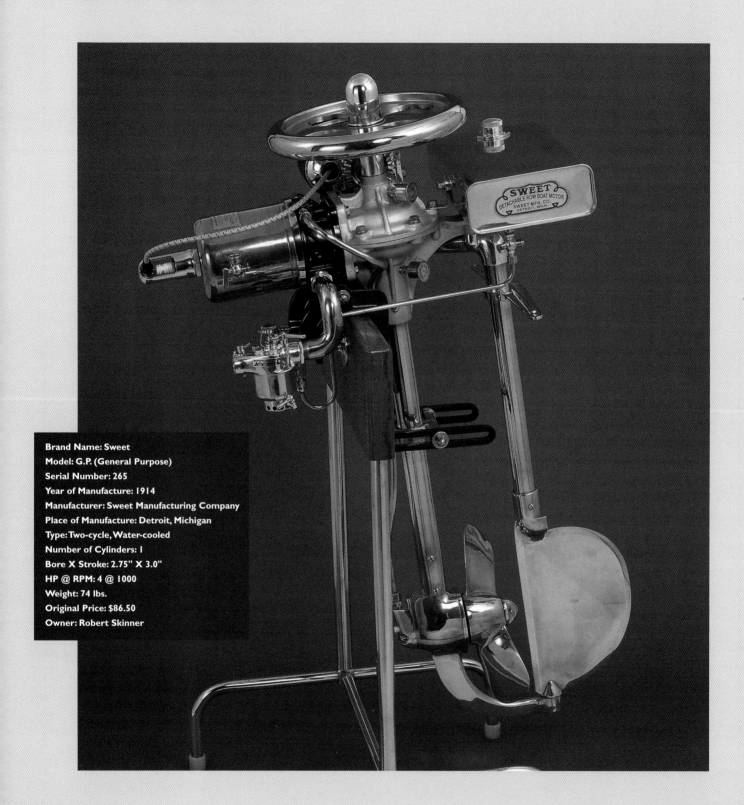

Brand Name: Sweet
Model: G.P. (General Purpose)
Serial Number: 265
Year of Manufacture: 1914
Manufacturer: Sweet Manufacturing Company
Place of Manufacture: Detroit, Michigan
Type: Two-cycle, Water-cooled
Number of Cylinders: 1
Bore X Stroke: 2.75" X 3.0"
HP @ RPM: 4 @ 1000
Weight: 74 lbs.
Original Price: $86.50
Owner: Robert Skinner

Just a stone's throw up Detroit's Griswold Street from Cameron Waterman's motor factory sat the Sweet Manufacturing Company. Within its brick walls, something took place that is considered mysterious by vintage outboard enthusiasts. Enigmatically, no one seems to recall exactly where Sweet outboards came from, and industrial historians will only speculate about the brand's origin. Some say its address simply denoted another entrance to the Waterman building. Whatever the truth, it appears that Sweet entered the outboard business in 1914. Period literature specifically states that the company "manufactures" outboard motors. Of course, that is not a surprising claim from a firm headlining "manufacturing company" in its name. Rather curious, though, is Sweet's close proximity to Waterman coupled with the fact that Sweet offered motors nearly identical to Waterman's. Then again, a single-cylinder Sweet has surfaced that was obviously a relabeled Evinrude Rowboat Motor. Certainly mystifying.

Normally, "badge-engineered" products vary from the maker's own brand only in some superficial, cosmetic fashion. And, such looks to be the case with the 1914 Sweet shown here. Its nuance differences from a 1914 Waterman include decals and a small identification tag affixed to the cylinder's copper water jacket cover. All other 1914 Sweet parts are interchangeable with that year's Waterman. Oddly enough, Sweet outboards appear to have a more generous horsepower rating — four instead of Waterman's three. Typically, it is the clone brand that gets tagged with subservient specs. Additionally, Sweet's range of options, such as reversing prop, magneto, and even a long shaft version, represent Waterman's latest advances.

Could it be that Sweet actually manufactured motors for Waterman, and that the Sweet name was placed on production overrun? The author feels such a twist is remotely possible, but unlikely given Waterman's incorrigible penchant for selling other companies privately branded Waterman Porto motors bearing only the thinnest of disguises. The Willis serves as early proof. In 1908, one E.J. Willis Company of New York advertised a "special fisherman's portable

rowboat motor" that was obviously a re-badged vertical cylinder Waterman. Another example is the World War One-era British Watermota. These Waterman clones were either exported ready-to-run to the United Kingdom, or might have been authorized knock-offs made with Waterman parts or licensed tooling. Watermota later made its own Waterman-like engines (inboard and outboard styles) claimed to be authorized by the British Admiralty. A Waterman bearing a London address has also surfaced. So the mystery deepens on two continents. In any event, precedent exists for antique outboard buffs to project that all Sweet kickers were produced by Waterman — except for that Evinrude clone. In fact, Sweet may have simply provided "middle man" marketing services, with all Sweet orders shipped directly from the Waterman plant. Ads for both companies — each with the identical line-drawn outboard graphic — were even known to show up on the same page of boating or outdoors magazines. Why make such an arrangement with a direct competitor who is just a short walk from your own business? Faced with meeting a payroll, what factory owner wouldn't be tempted to live by the axiom, "a sale is a sale."

Like the Waterman C-14, Sweet's 1914 model G.P. wore a fuel tank, steering bar, sparkplug guard, carburetor, intake manifold, rudder, propeller, lower unit, and crankshaft cap (above flywheel) formed from brass and bronze. The latter component also served as an oil-measuring cup to aid outboarders in properly mixing fuel. All that bronze and brass caused Sweet to promote its 1914 offering as a salt-water friendly model. In fact, musings among collectors of Watermans and Sweets reveal that — so far, anyway — all Waterman rudders are aluminum while Sweets use brass. Collectors of motors from this vintage are also fond of saying that it's easier to find a Sweet than a comparable Waterman. Either more of them were built than the related Waterman, or more survived the sea and scrap yard. When Cameron Waterman sold out in 1917, the Sweet brand disappeared from the market. It shouldn't really require a detective to solve any mystery in that.

Page opposite: Most every Sweet model had a Waterman "look-alike." Close observation of the two brands, though, typically shows that the Sweet employed brass where Waterman just used aluminum. The rudder and sparkplug guard serve as examples.

Joymotor, Racine, and Wilcox-McKim
EXOTIC COPYCATS

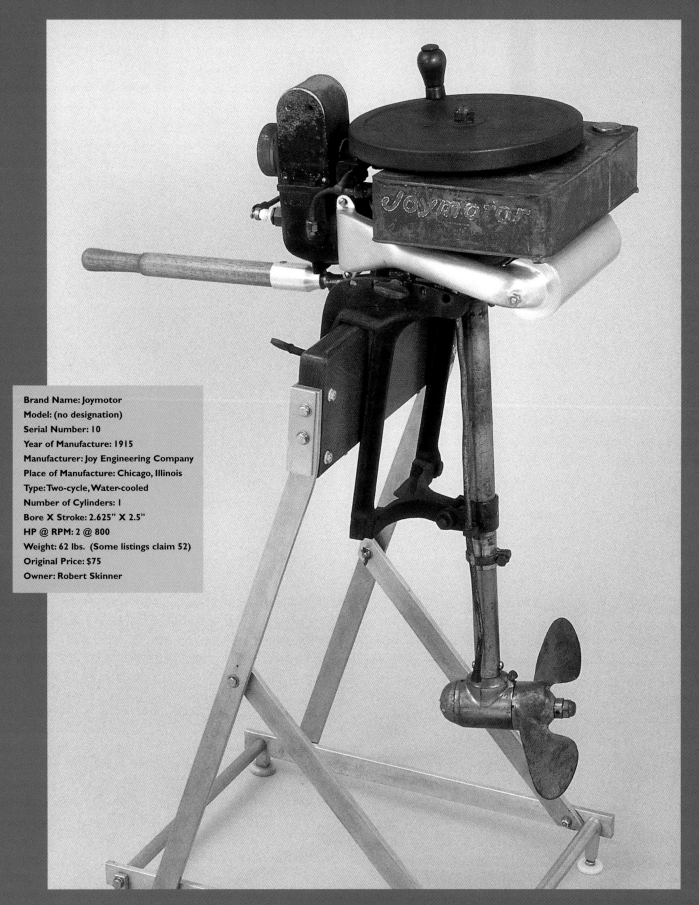

Brand Name: Joymotor
Model: (no designation)
Serial Number: 10
Year of Manufacture: 1915
Manufacturer: Joy Engineering Company
Place of Manufacture: Chicago, Illinois
Type: Two-cycle, Water-cooled
Number of Cylinders: 1
Bore X Stroke: 2.625" X 2.5"
HP @ RPM: 2 @ 800
Weight: 62 lbs. (Some listings claim 52)
Original Price: $75
Owner: Robert Skinner

During early 1916, *Motor Boating* magazine divulged an amazing fact. In an article titled *The Phenomenal Growth of the Outboard Motor,* it reported that "something like 300,000 outboard motors [were already then] in operation in [the United States] alone." While some 20 percent of them emanated from the busy Evinrude factory, and probably another 10 percent came through Waterman assembly lines, most were products of the fragmented outboard market that enjoyed a robust, short-lived, rather democratic shakedown from 1913 through America's entry into World War One. Literally dozens of firms entered the fray. In fact, many of the participating companies were quite ephemeral, lasting maybe a year or two around 1914-1916. Three, Joymotor, Racine, and Wilcox-McKim, are represented here.

Admittedly, Joymotors were bashfully offered through the early 1920s, but by then their heyday had long since passed. With virtually all national promotion during the first couple decades of the 20th Century being practically the sole province of small, inexpensive, half-tone or line-drawn advertisements in the likes of *The Rudder, Motor Boating,* and *Field & Stream,* each maker had a decent shot at gaining market share. All three companies' motors, albeit copying the successful forward-pointing single-cylinder Evinrude motif, wore enough other features to make each one unique. These oddities only serve to brighten the flash-in-the-pan effect that makes such "old iron" prized by vintage motor buffs today.

Among the countless racks of kickers in antique outboard collections, only a handful are home to a Joymotor. Surely, Chicago's Joy Engineering Company didn't intend to build museum artifacts when it began outboard production in 1915. The firm had secured a patent for a "reversing propeller" feature that would swing the lower unit 180 degrees by giving the tiller a hard right or left. It felt that such a luxury would soon become an outboarder's necessity and bring fortune to the license holder. Also of innovative note was Joymotor's water pump driven off of the cylinder-mounted magneto's linkage. This is one of the only powerhead-mounted water pumps that comes to mind. The pump was placed there to protect eyes from "unsightly, tangled up [water] pump hoses" that an Evinrude exhibited.

Other manufacturers followed the Waterman/Evinrude protocol of pumping from a unit on either the driveshaft or propeller shaft. Through a clamp screw, one could adjust, by five inches, the length of Joymotor's torque tube. Transom heights of this period were not typically cut for outboard use, consequently the variable feature seemed useful. For canoe owners, the Joymotor could be purchased with a "special bracket" that lowered the motor and made for a less "tippy" canoe. Black paint was applied to standard and canoe brackets, the cylinder was treated blue, and the fuel tank received a nice coat of red. With polished aluminum crankcase and exhaust manifold casting, as well as a bright nickel plating on the fuel line, water line, lower unit, and flywheel rim, the Joymotor would really stand out in any crowd of contemporaries. Maybe that's why early customers wrote to the company headquarters in the Chicago Tribune Building to glow, "Joymotor is rightly named" — "A joy to own" — "Evidently built to enjoy."

For reasons lost in time, though, the manufacturer couldn't sustain early successes. Oddly, the company wasn't even represented in the aforementioned *Motor Boating* outboard industry expose. It moved offices on several occasions and, before evaporating sometime in the early

On a vintage outboard, gear-driven, external (from flywheel) magnetos look like rather dubious contraptions. When in proper order though, they're capable of generating significant spark and eliminate the need to lug around batteries.

Fuel tank   Muffler   Steering gears   "Knuckle buster" starting knob   Mixing valve   Magneto

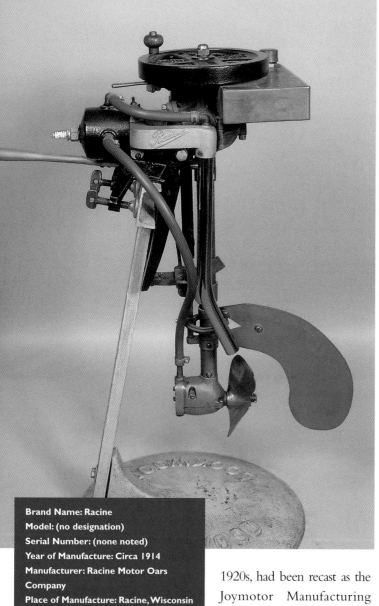

Brand Name: Racine
Model: (no designation)
Serial Number: (none noted)
Year of Manufacture: Circa 1914
Manufacturer: Racine Motor Oars Company
Place of Manufacture: Racine, Wisconsin
Type: Two-cycle, Water-cooled
Number of Cylinders: 1
Bore X Stroke: 2.62" X 3.12"
HP @ RPM: 2 @ 800
Weight: 65 lbs.
Original Price: $70
Owner: Robert Grubb

opportunity to clean out a back rack of grimy, obsolete motors. Often these hauls would net engines from makers fellow enthusiasts had never before known. Except for tiny, private jumbles of yellowed, company literature, and an obscure doctoral dissertation on the outboard industry, almost nothing had been written to help buffs identify the obscure fruit of their searches.

One of the most serendipitous finds happened to a New Jersey AOMC member who stopped at his local gas station for a sparkplug connector. Upon learning that the item would be used on an old outboard, the attendant offered his customer a vintage kicker dumped in a nearby barn. That led to the $12 purchase of the Racine pictured here. Over 30 years of lying on a moist dirt floor had rusted through the gas tank, but the rest of the Racine, much of it sand cast in bronze, remained remarkably intact. Using the skeleton of the old tank as a pattern, a new one was fabricated with .032" copper sheets. The tin rudder looked hopelessly homemade, so the restorer began searching for original Racine advertising that might yield clues. Another club member who had a shelf full of 1914-1915 boating publications discovered a couple of miniscule ads. Approximate dimensions of Racine's telltale semi-crescent rudder were estimated from these small depictions, and an educated guess replacement resulted.

Fresh black paint on the flywheel and cylinder castings highlighted the company venue and beautifully scripted logo. Information about this all but forgotten brand is still scarce, but the manufacturer appeared

1920s, had been recast as the Joymotor Manufacturing Company. As of this writing, serial number 10 in the rare series awaits her restoration. Even so, the old gal's patina earned by decades of survival provides her with an irreplaceable aura. A long lost muffler necessitated the location of a loaner from a sister motor so that a replacement part might be cast. In many cases, only two or three examples of these very rare brands exist, and spare components are virtually non-existent. That's where cooperative generosity, creativity and resourcefulness are most appreciated by collectors.

The Antique Outboard Motor Club's (AOMC) early days were marked by frequent discoveries. Especially during the1960s, a changing of the guard at many marine sales establishments meant that new, bottom-line-oriented owners were more than happy to find someone who'd actually pay them a few dollars for the

Lettering cast into the flywheel and the logo on the cylinder casting make Racine easy to identify. No serial or model numbers, though, were ever tagged on this rare rowboat motor. Racine's use of a simple "mixing valve" carburetor is typical of other brands during the mid-teens era. A "buzz coil," often liberated from a Model T Ford, and dry cell batteries provided ignition.

excited about promoting Racine's underwater exhaust tube, "making a perfect muffler." Also touted were a "special gasoline shut-off," and the fact that the motor could be started forwards or backwards and produce speeds of four- to eight-miles-per-hour. Apparently, sales never really picked-up, causing Racine to leave the market within a few years of its once hopeful introduction.

There's also little to go on when introducing the Wilcox-McKim outboard. Serial number 108 left Saginaw in 1914 and was orphaned two years later when its maker passed from the detachable rowboat motor business. Like the Racine, it wears a bronze underwater exhaust and lower unit. Neither does this engine care if it runs clockwise or counterclockwise. Relatively unusual is Wilcox-McKim's aluminum fly-wheel-mounted starting knob. As soon as the motor fires and the operator lets go of this handle, it drops into a flywheel-nesting cavity. The stationary knobs on ordinary outboards of the day were cursed as "knuckle-busters." Wilcox hoped that owners having kept their digits intact would spread the word about the fledgling marque. A few were among *Motor Boating's* 300,000 engine census. Today, in celebrated obscurity, the two or three survivors serve as worthy representatives from outboarding's first gold rush.

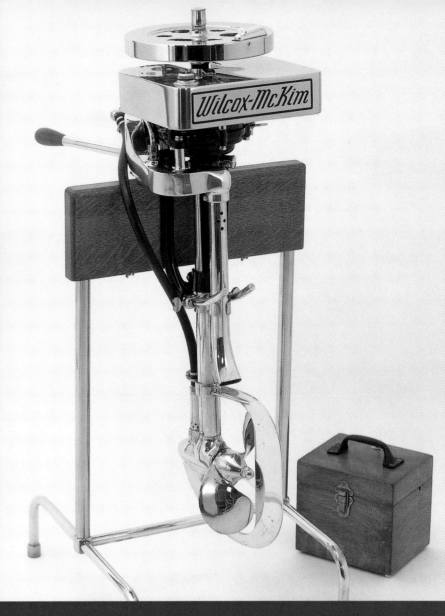

Brand Name:	Wilcox-McKim
Model:	(no designation)
Serial Number:	108
Year of Manufacture:	1914
Manufacturer:	Wilcox- McKim Company
Place of Manufacture:	Saginaw, Michigan
Type:	Two-cycle, Water-cooled
Number of Cylinders:	1
Bore X Stroke:	2.625" X 2.250"
HP @ RPM:	2.5 @ 900
Weight:	70 lbs.
Original Price:	about $75
Owner:	Robert Skinner

The brass fitting on top of Wilcox-McKim's flywheel is a grease cup. When filled and turned, it delivers lubrication to the top crankshaft bearing. Owners were told to give this item a twist several times during an average putt-putt down the lake.

The Motor with a Few True Fans

AEROTHRUST

Brand Name: Aerothrust 1914
Model: Metal Prop/High Tension Magneto
Serial Number: (none noted)
Year of Manufacture: 1914
Manufacturer: Aerothrust Engine Company
Place of Manufacture: Chicago, Illinois
Type: Two-cycle, Air-cooled
Number of Cylinders: 2
Bore X Stroke: 2.500" X 2.250"
HP @ RPM: 3 @ 1,800
Weight: 76 lbs.
Original Price: $85
Owner: Robert Skinner

High flying hyperbole was the stuff of early Aerothrust promotion. Ads in 1913 suggested that with an Aerothrust attached to a canoe, "60 miles per hour can be attained under favorable conditions." This represented quite a jump from a 1912 introductory press release promising just eight-mph. Even the company headquarters was all over the place, shifting Chicago addresses, then onto a couple more in La Porte, Indiana faster than its proverbial mile-a-minute canoe. Aerothrust was a novel idea looking for outdoors enthusiasts with imagination. In theory, much could be done with a portable airplane type powerplant. In fact, the firm's nascent advertising mentioned the distinct possibility of $20,000 in prizes to the first person to develop a "flying bicycle," and stated that such would be an "aviation experiment in which any bright American boy [using his trusty Aerothrust] may be the first to succeed." Indeed, it appears that the company's first focus was on biking enthusiasts as there were no doubt more of them than canoeists or rowboaters.

The initial (1913) Aerothrusts had one vertical, air-cooled cylinder cast in the same piece as the related crankcase. A "specially-designed carburetor [was] integral with the main motor casting." According to period literature, it was a design that originated from unnamed but "famous aviation experts." The package came with four mounting struts suitable for adapting, via customer-supplied bolts, to most any vehicle imaginable. Advertised at 11 pounds, this four horse @ 2,500 rpm mill might remind the casual observer of a large model airplane engine. Apparently, the inaugural version never took off. Artists' renditions, rather than actual photographs of the motor in ads, lead one to speculate some wishful thinking was in the air. And, nobody ever flew his bicycle to the Aerothrust factory for that prize money.

Motors did emanate from the plant in 1914. These were rotary valved, opposed-twin models with finned, air-cooled cylinders cast in a single piece along with the crankcase. Largely evaporated were suggestions to use the new Aerothrust on a bike. Its weight and height made two-wheeled association impractical. Instead, the company, touting itself as being "the largest manufacturer of aviation type motors in the world," aimed buyers at installing the Aerothrust on boats and ice sleds. Actually, a steering wheel-equipped, two-seat *Aero-Sled* was offered as an accessory unit for using the motor during winter. Regular boaters were promised an Aerothrust-powered hull could go anywhere the craft could float. This provided quite an advantage to shallow water mariners faced with rocks and weeds impacting conventional outboard lower units. Unfortunately, Aerothust designers — probably possessing an aviation mindset — didn't foresee the need to allow Aerothrust any lateral motion. Consequently an underwater rudder was needed for steering, defeating the air drive method's best characteristic.

Our subject 1914 Aerothrust is one of several styles the company issued through the early 1920s. It swings a 32-inch propeller of aluminum, while some are described as the alloy, "magnalium," evidently a mixture of magnesium and aluminum. Behind the prop hub, is a magneto. Mag versions are typically thought to be 1915 and later models, but this one was reportedly built in late 1914. From its brass fuel tank, either gasoline or kerosene may be burned. This provided a wonderful option in areas where good gas was unavailable.

Starting was facilitated by a removable hand crank that hooked into the non-prop end of the crankshaft. Also shown is 1915 Aerothrust model "D," serial number 2224. It has a 32-inch walnut prop and fires with the typical battery ignition set up of the day, a six-volt dry battery and Model "T" Ford buzz coil. For some reason, fuel tanks for most of these wooden-prop models were more rectangular than the slightly conical style of metal-propped Aerothrusts. Both of our featured Aerothrusts violate this rule with rectangular and cylindrical tanks. This simply demonstrates that the factory was capricious in following its own catalog descriptions. In fact, numerous variations of Aerothrust offerings — especially in fuel tank and muffler configurations — have surfaced, rather confounding antique engine buffs. A magneto version, with wood propeller, was offered, but utilized a conventionally sized outboard motor flywheel, mounted horizontally to face the operator. The crank method was continued here for starting.

Some of these engines have been found bearing the name Brooks. This concern purchased Aerothrust around 1917 after the original maker had taken up a Hoosier locale. There is also connection to the Pormo, but this was simply the brand of water pump accessory

A wooden prop 1915 Aerothrust Model "D," number 2224. While its fuel tank had a single cap and reservoir, some Aerothrusts had two, each with a valve and line leading to the carburetor. One could be filled with gasoline and the other with kerosene. This facilitated quick starting on the former, then switching to the latter, a fine feature in locales where gas was in short supply.

unit, said to deliver 125 gallons per minute with the three-horsepower Aerothrust (and small cooling fan blade) attached. A five-horse version got advertised, but is a rarity. Post-1916 Aerothrusts were given wooden laminated props with an increased blade pitch. This slowed RPM, but was said to increase boat speed and reduce engine wear. The company also began marketing a powerhead steering kit that allowed the motor to be turned via a steering handle, thus eliminating the need for a separate rudder arrangement.

Aerothrusts were inventively drafted for a variety of applications other than marine power. The author has heard of a 1919 model used by a farmer to blow stagnant summer air out of his dairy barn. A bevy of homebrew air-drive automobiles also utilized the Aerothrust. Although able to withstand its only major contemporary direct competitor, the Kemp Airdrive, (1918-1922), Aerothrust, along with its amusing advertising, quietly faded from the market around 1925.

It Ain't Heavy, It's My Koban

KOBAN

Brand Name: Koban
Model: "C"
Serial Number: 5851
Year of Manufacture: 1915
Manufacturer: Koban Manufacturing Company
Place of Manufacture: Milwaukee, Wisconsin
Type: Two-cycle, Water-cooled, Battery ignition
Number of Cylinders: 2
Bore X Stroke: 2.625" X 2.375"
HP @ RPM: 3 @ 800
Weight: 105
Original Price: $75
Owner: Robert Skinner

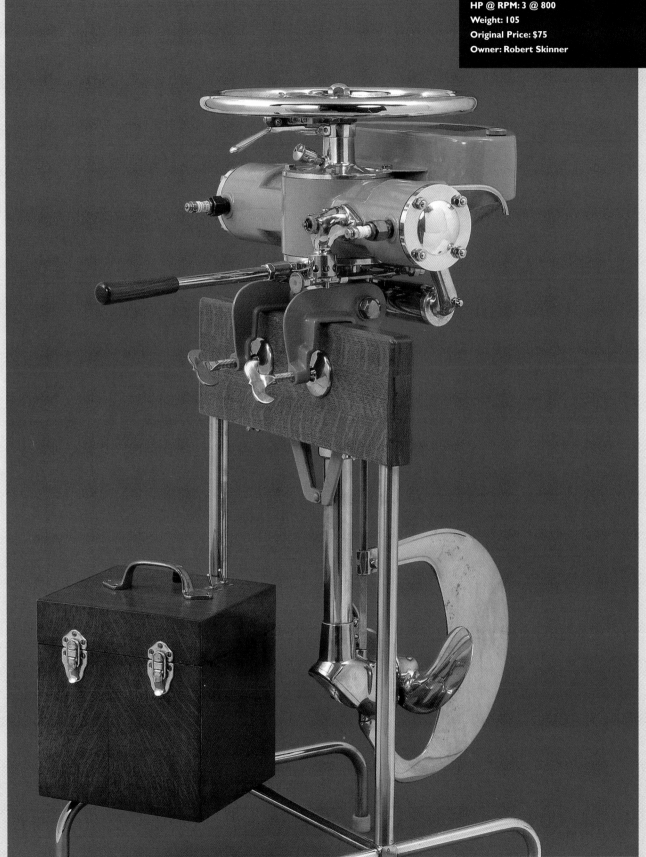

There was a word once loudly proclaimed as positive that causes the opposite reaction today — "husky." In pre-calorie counting America, someone who had a look of heaviness was thought to be much healthier than the once maligned thin individual. Even the label "fat cat" originated by the struggling proletariat in a spirit of jealousy for rich folk who obviously had more than enough to eat. Consequently, sheer bulk often symbolized strength. Lightness often meant flimsiness. Americans had recently celebrated President William Howard Taft, a chief executive so large that he required a custom jumbo bathtub at the White House. Koban weighed into the nascent outboard market while huskiness was almost universally valued.

To be fair, some of a Koban's mass can be attributed to the fact that it wore one more cylinder than 99 percent of its early competitors built on the Evinrude forward-pointing single motif. Koban Manufacturing Company founders, Arthur Koch and Walter Bannon — hence the *ko* and the *ban* — set out to offer a strong rowboat motor that could be easily distinguished from the rest. No doubt their Milwaukee venue allowed them to keep tabs on what co-located Evinrude was up to. It would be logical to assume that the duo felt outboard buyers were savvy enough to see that two cylinders could be better than one, especially in counter-balancing annoying engine vibration. Koch and Bannon also seemed to believe that consumers purchased mechanical goods while recalling the axiom, "heavier is better."

Most Kobans are monuments to solid brass, bronze, and cast iron. Strangely, though, many of this legion look like they're missing parts. Our 1915 subject engine serves as an example with few components breaking the lines of its twin cylinders and crankcase; all cast in one piece like the similar vintage Aerothrust. Period literature often mythologically touted Koban as the first two-cylinder outboard. This conveniently overlooked the obscure 1914 Aerothrust Federal, an even more ethereal twin version of the

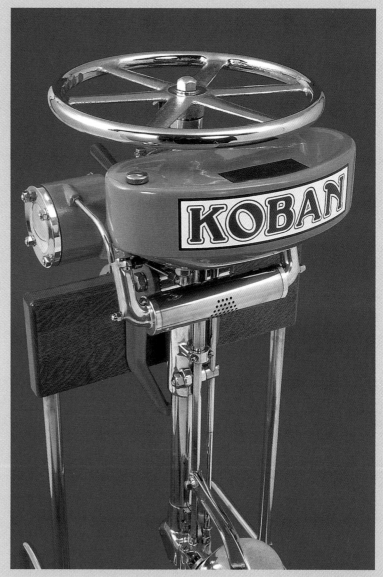

A Koban's fuel tank cap is dwarfed by the vintage twin's huge flywheel. For years, Koban brochures ridiculed other motor makers for equipping engines with unsafe knuckle busting, as well as potentially hand and arm breaking starting knobs. Of course, coming in contact with a whirling spoke or two from Koban's flywheel would hurt, too. By the late teens, Koban quietly surrendered to the knuckle-buster mode.

elusive 1898 American, and the Swedish brand Archimedes' 1912 twin. A more realistic claim is that it was the earliest with detachable cylinder heads, a nice feature not promoted by other makers until Johnson in 1929. Easily visible on the subject Koban is its top main bearing grease cup. Koban owner's manuals preached that operators should keep the cup well packed and give it a half turn — to inject extra lubrication into the vital bearing — every time the motor was run, even if for only a short outing. Another case of "more being better."

At an antique outboard meet, several casual observers commented on the Koban's interesting steering wheel. They logically mistook the rimmed fly-wheel for steering control, assuming it was somehow connected to the rudder. In fact, turning is facilitated by a tiller linked to the rudder. The flywheel's spoked-wheel shape was designed for a sure "grip and rotate" action that starts the engine. Through 1917, Koban bragged about not needing a knuckle-buster starting knob on its flywheels. By 1918, though, Kobans appeared with these erstwhile evils and then the ad rhetoric about other brands' starter handles suddenly disappeared. Also varied during Koban's production run were carburetor positioning, a magneto option, underwater exhaust, flywheel style, and from 1920, cylinders that detached from the crankcase. Later mod-els — especially due to their larger cylinder castings — appear even a bit bulkier than the first Kobans.

Certainly the Koban organization had satisfied cus-tomers and had some repeat business, although it's hard to imagine the hefty motors simply wearing out. Undoubtedly, Koban's bell began tolling around 1922 when other outboarders were seen easily toting their new 35-pound Johnson Light Twins, or trim Elto two-cylinder model. After all, to be practical, outboards are supposed to be portable. In the Great Gatsby flapper era, huskiness lost some of its charm. Featherweight aluminum components were fast replacing cast iron, brass, and bronze everyplace from cars to cookware. For some reason, even the group to which Koch and Bannon sold Koban didn't appreciate this trend. Advertisements for "the great 2-cylinder Koban row-boat motor" became less common by the mid-1920s, and vanished after Evinrude's 1926 buyout of the once grand company. No matter, it is likely Evinrude offered Koban owners some spare parts, as well as also build-ing a few complete Kobans for sale as "specials." Several Koban employees were included in the takeover booty. One didn't retire from Evinrude until having helped put together the company's helpful model/year motor identification guide during the late 1950s. Long respected at the Evinrude plant as an *old Koban man,* he reminded younger employees about the days when any outboard marketed as a quality product had to be cast with the spirit of "huskiness" in mind.

Outboarding's Big Tip
FEDERAL

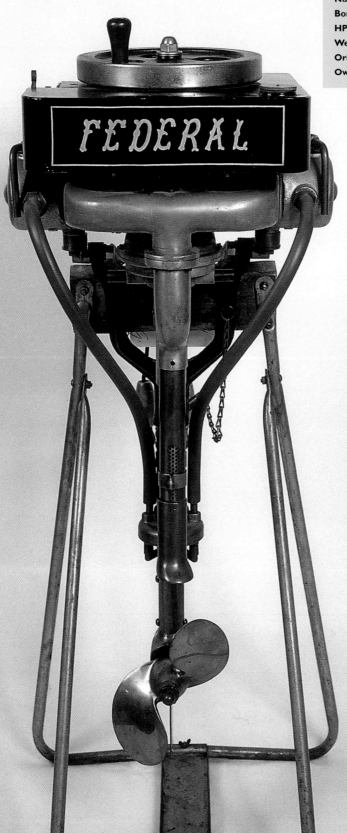

Brand Name: Federal
Model: Twin
Serial Number: 9515A
Year of Manufacture: circa 1915
Manufacturer: Federal Motor and Manufacturing
   Company
Place of Manufacture: Newark, New Jersey
Type: Two-cycle, Water-cooled
Number of Cylinders: 2
Bore X Stroke: 2.750 X 2.500
HP @ RPM: 3 @ 1,200
Weight: 90 lbs.
Original Price: NA
Owner: Robert Grubb

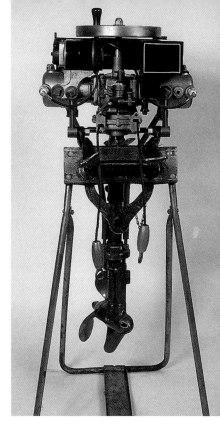

Two very simple brainstorms provided great conveniences for outboarders. The first occurred when a two-cycle engine owner got tired of constantly filling and monitoring his motor's thirsty drip oilers. During the first few years of two-stroke technology's existence, operators poured straight gasoline in the fuel tank and then dribbled the needed oil into those little glass and metal lubricators. A now forgotten fellow simply mixed the two together in his engine's tank. Word spread when all went well. Another resourceful fellow, tired of having to remove his outboard from the boat whenever beaching the craft, thought to loosen the lower unit angle-adjust bolt and tilt up the kicker. This now seems like a logical feature, but it took most outboard makers years to see such light. Even as late as the mid-1920s Evinrude, for example, specially identified some of their rowboat motors with a "T" (for "tilt") at the end of serial number. The Federal Motor and Manufacturing Company boasted its own tilting outboard in 1915. Also worthy of mention is Federal's twin-cylinder format, a then novel outboard motor configuration largely credited to more prominent rival Koban.

A bit of mystery must be included with the Federal story. The short-lived Washington, DC-based motor maker appears to have instigated two other unusual brands that boasted twins, Arrow and National. Our subject engine came from the company's Newark, New Jersey plant around 1915. The factory was said to have begun outboard production the year before. By 1916, Newark's Arrow Motor and Machine Company, Inc., (its factory operated in Jersey, but the firm was headquartered in New York) offered a four-horse twin with an undeniable resemblance to the Federal. There's little doubt of a relationship. Simultaneously, another suspiciously similar two-cylinder outboard, the National, materialized from the National Marine Motor Company, also of Newark. It appears Arrow tried to improve Federal's standard transom thumb-screws by substituting an ingenious push-down lever while National employed a church collection plate-style flywheel with a wide rim for hand-spin starting. Both successor models featured variable-pitch propellers. None of the three firms grabbed much market share. National was gone by 1919, with the Arrow twin limping along not much longer.

Much historical research of World War One-era minor-make outboards is done with the brand's one or two known surviving motors, which are often enigmatically different in some confounding fashion. Other tools of the trade are period boating magazines' annual motor listings, and tiny ads possibly blessed with an artist's rendering of the product. These sources must understandably be studied with the knowledge that former engine owners might have added, subtracted, or modified the outboard. Then, too, advertising descriptions and manufacturers' lists were

Federal used a double-capacity water pump to provide cooling for twice the number of cylinders offered by most of its competitors. Rope could be tied to the steering pull knobs in order to allow the operator to be seated in the middle or front seat.

very susceptible to fudging. Such study makes possible any number of scenarios. Perhaps, Arrow made the Federal motors all along, but took over the line because of some conflict with Federal? Perhaps National was a sister brand actually controlled by Arrow? Suffice it to say there's lots of opportunity for speculation.

Our photographed engine offers almost the sole palpable evidence of the series. This Federal exhibits features described in a 1915 ad showing: handles on the steering cable to rotate the lower unit from forward to reverse, gear driven Bosch high tension magneto (battery ignition model also available), vertically adjustable shaft to accommodate various transom heights, tilting lower unit with lock that automatically disengages if severe obstruction is encountered, underwater exhaust and cut-out, steel transom bracket instead of typical cast iron, and double capacity plunger-type water pump "so that motor is always cool enough to handle." A New Jersey outboard enthusiast not far from Newark found our subject motor in the 1960s. If the Federal could talk, no doubt this unique kicker would tell of the long ago day when its original owner chose it because of all the good ideas it so beautifully featured.

Good Brand, Bad Motor

EVINRUDE 4-CYCLE

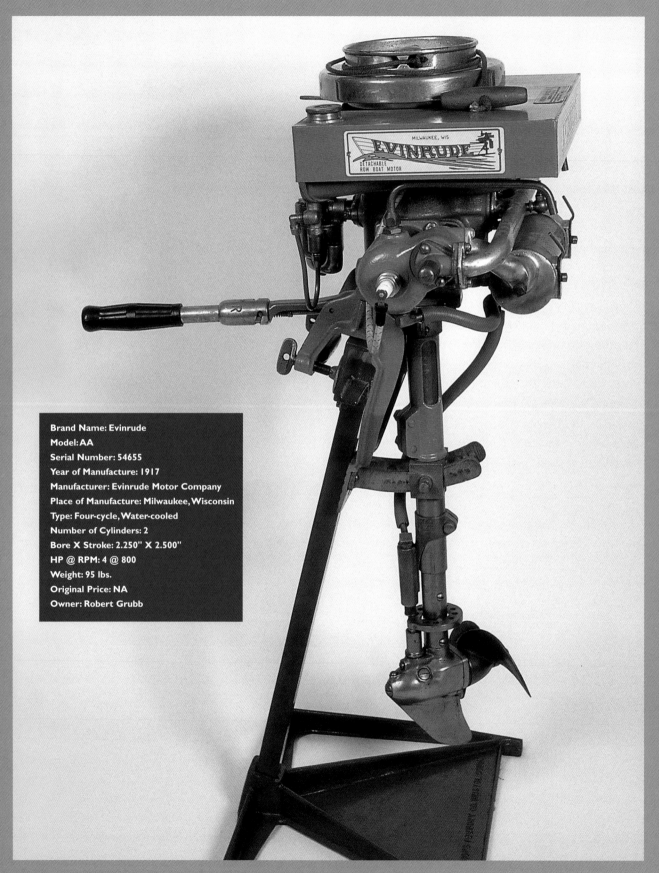

Brand Name: Evinrude
Model: AA
Serial Number: 54655
Year of Manufacture: 1917
Manufacturer: Evinrude Motor Company
Place of Manufacture: Milwaukee, Wisconsin
Type: Four-cycle, Water-cooled
Number of Cylinders: 2
Bore X Stroke: 2.250" X 2.500"
HP @ RPM: 4 @ 800
Weight: 95 lbs.
Original Price: NA
Owner: Robert Grubb

Ole Evinrude probably would not have allowed a single model AA Twin to leave the factory. But, in 1916, he wasn't a part of the company that bore his name. Consequently, some outboarders blamed a man who had nothing to do with the balky boat motor they had hoped would be twice as good as the trusty Evinrude single. After all, Ole's erstwhile organization headlined his moniker in announcing the new four-cycle detachable. "Here it is at last — the detachable rowboat motor you have been waiting for! A two-cylinder, opposed four-cycle EVINRUDE. You know the Evinrude name and reputation — first for years among detachable rowboat motors." Because Evinrude Model AA owners were often removing their engines for troubleshooting, little facetious license would be needed by competitors to joke that the term "detachable" — as opposed to "attachable" — was the debut announcement's operative word.

To be fair, it should be acknowledged that this outboard represented the proverbial "old college try." Post-Ole Evinrude officials were doing OK selling the basic singles that the company founder had designed in 1909, but they recognized a need to begin branching out. Beginning in 1914, the firm championed flywheel magnetos, rather than gear-driven, external units. While certainly not delivering as consistently a hot a spark as modern mags, these became successful enough so that other makers copied the concept. Some even bought Evinrude magneto systems to offer on their own brands. No doubt, Evinrude execs took note when cross-town rival, Koban, started moving respectable quantities of Koban twins. There must have been some resolve at Evinrude not to be outdone. Maybe, in this spirit of one-upmanship the decision was made to offer not just a twin-cylinder Evinrude, but an entirely new outboard truly based on mechanical principles so revered in the automotive realm . . . namely, the four-cycle engine.

In July, 1967, the late Toronto, Ontario dentist and marine propulsion historian, James L. Smith, aptly described this motor's construction for the *Antique Outboarder*:

"The powerhead being stationary, steering is accomplished as the tiller bar rotates [only] the lower unit. The forward-reverse feature used in the single cylinder model similarly is retained. Gas is fed from the tank to a large brass French-made Solex carburetor. This carburetor alone weighs two pounds, fourteen ounces, and is very well made, having float feed, choke and throttle valves. The gaseous mixture is fed directly into the large cylindrical crankcase, thence out the rear past the camshaft and into the exterior mounted intake manifold. This is nothing more than a round aluminum pipe and is equipped with a petcock for priming purposes. The pipe is attached at either end to a bronze intake valve housing. To the rear of each cylinder, and cast integral with it, is a chamber which fills with the gaseous vapor mixture during the intake stroke. To one side is attached the housing containing the intake valve, to the other side is fitted the exhaust valve. This chamber which is filled alternately with intake and exhaust gases opens by a single port into the cylinder and in reality forms a portion of the combustion chamber during the operation of the motor. The bronze intake valve housing may be seen in the picture [of our subject motor] as a pipe-like projection, straight out from the cylinder and just to the rear of the sparkplug. Within [this] housing is the valve and spring. Suction created during the intake stroke is sufficient to overcome the tension of the spring, [therefore] the valve opens. When the intake stroke is complete, spring pressure again closes the valve. The exhaust valves, however, are mechanically operated. A camshaft is accommodated in a portion of the crankcase extending rearward and the camshaft gear meshes with a gear mounted on the upper portion of the crankshaft. Eccentrics on the camshaft then operate a pair of pushrods which in turn activate the exhaust valves fitted in the common chamber previously described. Valves are spring returned and the whole system is timed to take its proper sequence in the cycle."

One would think it wise to offer four-cycle Evinrude owners a trade-off for all the inherent complexity and weight associated with such a system. Over the years, makers of four-cycle outboards have cited fuel economy and the freedom from having to worry about fooling with oil at every gas fill-up. Unfortunately, Evinrude engineers couldn't figure out how to get straight lubrication from an automotive-like crankcase oil reservoir and into areas of friction. Company public relations people did their best to smooth over the problem with a press release that they gave 1916 *Motor Boating* editors.

"Perhaps the most unique feature in the construction of the motor," the magazine relayed to its readers, "is the oiling system. Due to the fact that the crankshaft

This motor was dealer-fitted with an accessory rope sheave that allowed removal of the knuckle-buster knob in favor of a pull cord. Note valve rod covers near sparkplugs.

Evinrude struggled with these engines for two model years before dropping them in 1918. When the firm returned to making twin-cylinder rowboat motors via its model L series four-horse twin in 1923, it was sure to release it in a traditional two-cycle format. That same year, Evinrude truly made amends with two-cylinder outboard shoppers by offering a nice-running, compact, 2.5 hp, Model N series Sportwin. By this time, Ole was back in business manufacturing his second great motor, the ELTO Ruddertwin, and probably expressed some relief that his old company, albeit a direct competitor, finally marketed a twin worthy of the Evinrude name.

stands in a vertical position, with the cranks traveling in a horizontal plane, and for other reasons peculiar to outboard motor design, the ordinary [four-cycle] method of splash or force feed lubrication was found to be insufficient. The oil, therefore, is mixed with the gasoline which is taken in through the crankcase, as in the common practice with small two-cycle motors. However, a different principle is involved in this case, as there is no necessity for crankcase compression, and a check valve in the carburetor is used only to keep the [carb] from leaking gasoline."

Waiving the crankcase pressure was little reward for all the springs, valves, cam, and mixing gas with oil. The latter was arguably the chief complaint of two-stroke engine owners, so to pitch this requirement to four-cycle Evinrude buyers as well, seems questionable. Of course, the bottom line query for most outboarders is: *How well will this new model typically start?* Pointing to the "knuckle buster knob mounted on the heavy [Evinrude AA] flywheel," Smith paints a frustrating picture. "The engine has a crude magneto with points attached exteriorly on the spark retard [and advance] lever. With the weak ignition system [exacerbated by the era's poor magnets], the devious and complicated fuel induction system, together with the difficult cranking pressure against two cylinders, starting would present a real problem at times, requiring a supreme combination of stout hearted optimism and patience."

Although opposed-cylinder outboards typically fired their spark plugs simultaneously, the Evinrude four-cycle model was set up to fire its twin cylinders alternately.

Vive La Difference!

AMPHION

Brand Name: Amphion
Model: Twin Vertical Cylinder Outboard
Serial Number: 1032
Year of Manufacture: circa 1920
Manufacturer: Clarence J. Allen
Place of Manufacture: Milwaukee, Wisconsin
Type: Two-cycle, Water-cooled
Number of Cylinders: 2
Bore X Stroke: 63.5 mm X 63.5 mm (approximately 2.500" square)
HP @ RPM: 4 @ 900
Weight: 80 lbs.
Original Price: $115 (in 1922)
Owner: Robert Grubb

Originally designed as an inboard motor, this French connection "moteur universel" engine was nicely adapted by Amphion to outboard mode. Its transmission and shift lever are noted near the rear-mounted magneto. Starting is facilitated by giving the flywheel a vigorous spin… or two.. or three.

Two persons are associated with one of the most unusual two-cylinder outboards of the industry's formative period. Identifying which one actually pioneered the clever Amphion twin, however, will likely always be open to speculation. That's because period boating magazine listings and descriptions of Amphion don't exactly mesh with a detailed account of its obscure origin made decades ago by one of Evinrude's most respected executives. He begins Amphion history with a Mr. Clarence J. Allen who worked with Ole Evinrude during the early 1910s. Reportedly, Allen tooled-up a couple of small inboard marine engines (a single and twin), then recalled Ole's expanding success in the detachable market. Wishful thinking (in 1915) caused him to adapt the two-cylinder model onto an outboard lower unit. The resulting Amphion brand motors went on sale as the first alternate-firing outboards. They also boasted other innovative features such as tilting, magneto ignition, and forward/reverse transmission.

According to the story, Amphion twins were available through 1919, with Allen selling out remaining inventory to fellow Milwaukee resident, A.J. Machek, during the 1920s. Intrigue enters in the form of a 1916 *Motor Boating* description for the very motors Allen was said to have developed. Nowhere is his name mentioned. In fact, the outboard was identified as the Machek-Amphion and, in the magazine's narrative, its "general design is declared to follow closely with the best French practice, and . . . the cylinders are bored in accordance with French measurements."

Understandably, this French connection makes one question the *made by a little old Milwaukee machinist* angle. Perhaps the powerplants or their design came from France or Quebec? Allen enters the literature by 1922 through a listing in April 23rd *MotorBoat's* "Marine Motors Built in the USA." There, he is noted as the manufacturer of a twin-cylinder inboard and the Amphion outboard. The author notes that a broadcasting annual continued listing him as owner of an FM radio station years after he sold it, and suggests that even well meaning publishers of rosters can be inaccurate.

Our subject model wears the name C. J. Allen-Amphion cast into the cylinder assembly. It also sports the very French wording, "Moteur Universel." So, if the magazines can be trusted, it hails from about 1920.

The 1032 serial number might indicate that about 200 motors were built per year from 1916-1920. This seems to be in accordance with output of minor makes that often operated on an almost as-per-order basis. Then again, the digits may not hold any long-range significance. No matter the origin, this Amphion occupies an honored place in one of America's finest outboard collections.

The owner, once the holder of Mercury Marine's oldest dealer franchise, has hundreds of running motors at his disposal and counts the pictured Amphion as his favorite. Its unorthodox powerhead format (vertical cylinders), exposed Bosch magneto, transmission/gearshift lever, rudder, and prominent "hand spin start" flywheel, give Amphion real antique appeal. The tilt feature and relative smoothness of alternate firing twin cylinders make it a pleasure to run.

It would be nice to close with an exact end date for the unique Amphion. But, both the vintage literature and stories get hazy by the mid-1920s. The author is led to believe that Allen de-emphasized the vertical twin, began offering a more conventional opposed-cylinders twin, and then sold his business. Around 1928, whomever controlled the Amphion name had parts cast for a six-horse, opposed-twin dubbed Dreadnought. The motors were simply designated: models 5, 5A, 6, and 7. Amphion catalogs of this period always included weights in kilos and piston displacements in cubic centimeters, hinting of a foreign connection. Even in the US and Canada, though, few hit the market.

In the late 1960s, an AOMC member happened upon an unfinished Dreadnought along with sundry parts. The find was represented to him as the successor company's remnants. There are also end-game tales of some Amphion stock being donated by yet another Amphion rights holder to a Milwaukee area high school several years after World War Two. Like the checkered genealogies of many small outboard marques, all this simply adds to the Amphion Vertical Twin's mystique.

KNIGHT

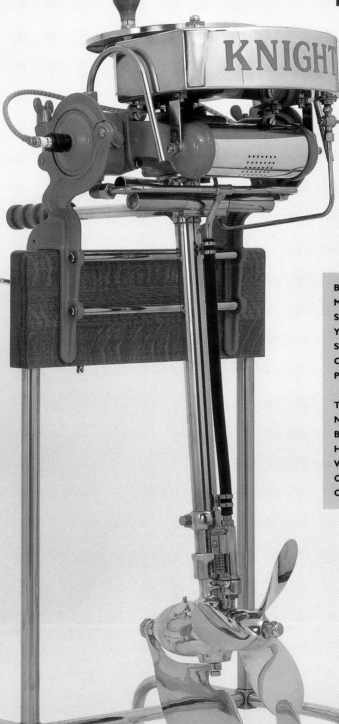

Brand Name: Knight
Model: Balanced Twin
Serial Number: 1774
Year of Manufacture: 1917
Sales Organization: The "Knight" Outboard Motor
Company, Ltd.
Place of Sale: Riverside, Hampton Wick, Kingston-
   on-Thames, England
Type: Two-cycle, Water-cooled
Number of Cylinders: 2
Bore X Stroke: 50 mm X 50 mm
HP @ RPM: 2.5 @ 1,100
Weight: 75 lbs.
Original Price: $70
Owner: Robert Skinner

It certainly seems proper to assume that an industrious, seafaring nation like England would spawn some of the world's first outboard motor makers. After all, every resident of the British Isles is never further than about 50 miles from ocean, river, or lake. And, early on, UK manufacturers began creating many of the world's finest automobile and motorcycle marques. Curiously, though, it appears most all of the first outboards in British territory were made elsewhere. The "Knight" Balanced Twin serves as one example.

English outboarding started with imports from France and America. Some of Cameron Waterman's 1911-1914 motors were sold through the Hampton Wick, Middlesex concern, Walter D. Fair & Company. Reportedly, the Royal Navy secured a few of these and was enough pleased with the kickers to request more. When, for some reason, Fair's direct import agreement with Waterman ended around 1913-1914, the Admiralty is said to have urged Fair to manufacture a British outboard. A Waterman C-16 (3-4 hp) lookalike dubbed WaterMota Mark I resulted, officially making England an outboard motor producing country. During the 1920s, at least a dozen domestic names were competing with Fair's WaterMota, which eventually stretched its Waterman-based single-cylinder powerhead design to an amazing 15 horsepower for racing purposes.

Meanwhile, the "Knight" Outboard Motor Company, Ltd., developed a modest business via the import of an opposed twin made by the Archimedes Company of Sweden. Actually, Archimedes got the design from two inventive brothers, Oscar and Alrik Hult, who encountered the 1910 Evinrudes that made their way from Milwaukee, Wisconsin, to Scandinavian fishermen. The Swedish duo decided to develop their own outboard, but with two cylinders. This work enabled Archimedes to introduce a notably reliable twin in 1912. One can project that Mr. Knight observed the success of WaterMota, and might have seen an early Archimedes happily pushing some English rowboat up the Thames. In any event, sometime in the mid-teens he connected with the Archimedes people and arranged for them to build a thinly disguised British version of the Swedish outboard. As expected in badge-engineering cases, comparison of the two (Swedish vs. English) appears to yield only a few cosmetic differences. There's the "Knight" nomenclature on the fuel tank and the ornately cast identification of the "Knight's" flywheel. This knuckle-buster bedecked disc, along with the fuel tank, exhaust can, tiller, water pump, lower unit, propeller, skeg, carburetor — as well as the water and fuel lines — are all brass or bronze. This makes for one potentially stellar finish. Of course, even Mr. Knight's personal motor probably wasn't as beautifully treated as our example, the restorer having devoted some 320 hours to the project. Notable "Knight" features include its oversized lower unit skeg, remarkably wide transom clamp bracket, large three-blade prop, and two ignition coils (one for each cylinder) instead of the single coil typically fitted to simultaneously-firing opposed twins.

A roadblock of dead ends relating to the final years of most small, long-ago ventures is at work here, so it's unclear exactly why and when Mr. Knight's firm ceased operation. Some of his final advertising items in the author's file dates from 1923, showing a motor apparently identical to the one in our photographs. Urgent pleas, such as, "Do not buy an outboard motor before trying a 'Knight," and "Do not delay buying until you want to use the motor," received the advert's largest point size. Part of the "Knight" (always presented inside quotation marks) Outboard Motor Company's promotion contained the offer; "We give trial runs with any of our models at any season of the year." Readers picturing a harsh Dickensonian December might imagine how taking that opportunity literally might force some old beleaguered London "Knight" dealer — bony fingers protruding from torn gloves — to dodge ice in the River Thames. But, the real question rises from the ad's inference that there were, indeed, other "Knight" models. Maybe Mr. Knight imported and the private-branded motors from makers other than Archimedes? Perhaps a bigger carb/crankcase opening made for a version with slightly more horsepower? Then again, "any of our models" might mean a battery ignition version, or simply engines of various color schemes? No matter, It looks like "Knights" were not marketed past the mid- to late 1920s. By then, lots of England's outboard shoppers automatically gave their allegiance to the many exciting, speedy, and readily available exports from the USA.

Two Pulls Will Convince You

CAILLE 5-SPEED WITH REWIND START

Brand Name: Caille
Model: 5-Speed Rowboat Motor with Rewind Starter
Serial Number: 34952
Year of Manufacture: probably 1920
Manufacturer: Caille Perfection Motor Company
Place of Manufacture: Detroit, Michigan
Type: Two-cycle, Water-cooled
Number of Cylinders: 1
Bore X Stroke: 2-5/8 X 2-1/2
HP @ RPM: 2 @ 700
Weight: 72 lbs.
Original Price: $90
Owner: Robert Grubb

There wasn't a pioneer outboard maker alive who didn't dream of offering the world's easiest starting motor. While other manufacturers were fooling around with shapes of flywheel-mounted "knuckle-buster" knobs and debating between rim-hand start or wrap-around rope, Caille introduced a convenient rewind starter. This 1916 outboard accessory was nearly two decades ahead of its time, and so revolutionary that it had to be explained in large print. "You don't crank this motor," Caille's full page May 1916 *Motor Boating* ad announced. "Anybody — man, woman or child — can easily, safely and conveniently start this universally acknowledged leader among rowboat motors. Takes less effort to lift than a two pound box of candy. It has the simplest, surest, most reliable and practical starter ever produced. It's purely mechanical and can't fail. The Caille Starter is mounted on top of the flywheel and engages the motor shaft by a simple coil and ratchet. The operator takes hold of a small handle on a coiled strap, gives a quick pull and the flywheel immediately revolves like a top. Means no more blistered hands, no more aching arms from cranking, no more knocks from a revolving cranking handle–no more catching of clothing."

This well-greased mechanism allowed the Caille owner to feather the motor's propeller via linkage to the steering arm. Up or down motion made the prop move through five speeds — more correctly, five pitch settings — from fast reverse to fast forward. Caille counted neutral as a "speed." A button on the end of the tiller had to be depressed when changing such prop pitch.

Spiffy dressers, Adolph and Arthur Caille (pronounced "Kale") added inboard marine engines to their manufacturing and movie theater endeavors in 1910. This was just a few years after the duo's foundry was said to have filled an order for some outboard motor parts castings placed by fellow Detroit resident Cameron Waterman. By 1913, the brothers' Caille Perfection Motor Company had its own outboard in the catalog. The debut Caille kicker borrowed largely from contemporaries with the knuckle-buster, rudder steering, and above water muffler can. Even with a generically mixed identity, it sold well enough for the Caille brothers to begin extending this outboard into a product line of several unique motors. A penchant for gadgetry sprang from their successes building rather

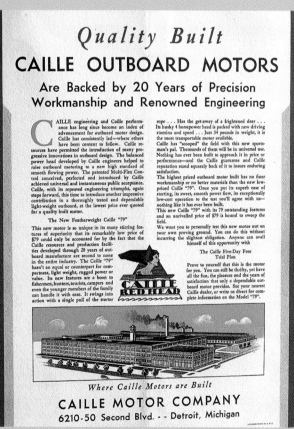

elaborate coin-operated machines the likes of an intricate slot machine with several jackpots and the capacity to accommodate a dozen players. Soon, depictions of some of pioneer outboarding's most exotic gizmos were appearing in Caille ads. Our featured motor wears two of the most useful, the rewind starter and a five-speed, variable pitch propeller.

Starter Starts It
No Cranking
Simply Pull This Strap

In the early 20th Century, any marine powerplant touted to possess "automotive" features was considered well endowed. Boat engines equipped with automotive type carburetors serve as a "for instance." Caille hit upon a natural car/outboard connection when comparing a motor vehicle's transmission to its outboards' five-speed option. In fact, Caille seemed to be offering a much greater range of shifting possibilities than Henry Ford did with his wildly popular Model "T" car. Of course, one of Caille's speeds was actually the not too speedy position known as neutral. The other four consisted of high-speed forward, trolling, slow reverse, and backward fast. "All speed [shift] changes," Caille ads instructed, "are made without stopping, reversing [the lower unit] or altering the speed of the motor, by simply pushing a button at the end of the steering handle."

Potential buyers might have envisioned a Caille 5-Speed shifting past the shoreline and sounding like an eager motorcycle accelerating through its gearbox, but motion changes in this outboard were relatively docile. Still, the variable pitched propeller feature accumulated a respectable customer base. Caille wasn't the only maker offering a feathering prop, but seemed to have the best franchise. As far as most of the outboard buying public was concerned, it neutralized variable pitch competitors such as Waterman, Sweet, and Federal. Then the gadget-loving company went into high gear putting the "5-Speed" propeller system on most all of its subsequent top of the line outboards, up to a 1930s, 23 horsepower model.

Caille's rewind never made this transition to many of the firm's other motors. Listings indicate engines similar to the one pictured disappeared from the literature around 1925. While the rewinder was impressively designed for 1916, the catalog claim that it "can't

fail," itself failed to factor in long-armed pulling, typical powerhead idiosyncrasies, and hotheaded human nature. The method didn't really catch on in the industry until well into the thirties, after scores of chewed-up rewind pawls and uncooperative springs had sent confounded engineers from every leading outboard manufacturer back to drawing board. Even then, more than a few outboarders experienced that proverbial telltale "ratchety-snap" noise and a related grease-inked rewind starting cord that refused to return to from whence it came. Consumers were loath to pay for an option that they'd heard would surely fail, leaving them with plain old wrap-a-rope start — but no usable rope.

Even electric starting Caille outboards, arriving in 1930, flopped. But, rather quickly, so did everyone else's during that era. They were a maze of easily overheated wires, and had not been sufficiently field-tested by Caille, Evinrude, Johnson, nor supplier Owens-Dyneto. A similar fate befell inertia starters designed by Bendix Eclipse Aviation Corporation. They had a push-button release that caused a spring-loaded ratchet drive to spin the flywheel. Like other outboard makers, Caille got stung on that sure-fire, outsourced item, too. The Caille brothers certainly had a lively idea in their rewind starter, though. It simply took longer than expected to engage the boating public. By 1946, many small outboards were ordered with this easy starting feature. Word spread that the new generation rewinder usually rewound OK. Just a few years later, any motor without one was considered to be a potential nightmare.

CAILLE LIBERTY DRIVE

Brand Name: Caille
Model: LD 19 (Liberty Drive Single)
Serial Number: 34832
Year of Manufacture: 1919
Manufacturer: Caille Perfection Motor Company
Place of Manufacture: Detroit, Michigan
Type: Two-cycle, Water-cooled, Battery ignition
Number of Cylinders: 1
Bore X Stroke: 2,625" X 2.500"
HP @ RPM: 2 @ 700
Weight: 68 lbs.
Original Price: $65
Owner: Robert Skinner

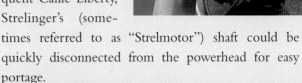

Someone important at Caille had rather lousy premonitions. In 1917, he authorized admen to "predict that ere long the old vertical type (of outboard) will be pretty much a novelty on lakes and streams as a horse and carriage on the boulevards." Caille was betting part of the farm on a direct-drive outboard that required no lower unit gears, and could be used in shallow water. Dubbed the "Liberty Motor," it was supposed yield freedom to boaters tired of having to drop a motor from dock to transom or being forced balance the kicker on the stern seat and then row to deep enough water to properly clamp it. Oddly, the outboard industry was about 15 years old before the idea of tilt-up motors caught on, so rowboat motors that could be swung above the waterline while affixed to a transom were rare.

Caille Liberty advertising spoke to those who never again wanted to tangle with securing a non-tilt "old vertical" (as the company pooh-poohed the genre) motor. "Now," their literature said with relief, "the danger of falling into the water while leaning far over the stern of the boat to attach your motor, is over. The Caille Liberty Motor can be attached on land. Then you just shove your boat out in the water, give the flywheel a turn, and zip! off you go." Sounds like a no-brainer today, but try obtaining such convenience with a motor that can't tilt.

The Detroit manufacturer didn't introduce the direct-drive or straight shaft outboard modus operandi. That was already old hat, having been done in the previous century by the Salisbury and Allen Portable Electric Propeller people. During the early 1900s, a French outboard called "Motogodille" was making waves with the design. And, another Detroit manufacturer, Strelinger Marine Engine Company, introduced its "Portable Boat = Drive," with an equal sign trademark designating the straight-shaft outboard mode, (models from 2 to 5 hp) in 1914. The author believes cross-town Caille took positive note of Strelinger's obscure product and may have even compensated them in some way, as it appears Strelinger direct-drive outboards' 1916 departure cleared the way for Caille to take credit for the concept in its 1917 Liberty Drive debut literature. A check of vintage Strelinger ads shows that, just as Caille would later do, the small firm focused upon "that serious defect in small motors heretofore," when comparing its direct-drive outboard

to conventional ones of vertical drive-shaft/non-tilt design. Also like the subsequent Caille Liberty, Strelinger's (sometimes referred to as "Strelmotor") shaft could be quickly disconnected from the powerhead for easy portage.

To be sure, Caille championed direct-drive outboarding more aggressively than anyone else did. In fact it didn't take long for direct-drive outboards of any variety to often be referred to as "Liberty Drive" motors. Caille catalogs stayed with the Liberty Single, in various incarnations, from 1917 to 1931. No doubt, leftovers could be had well into the Great Depression.

The garden tool-type handle was supplied by Caille as a handy Liberty Drive accessory. When easy portage was required, the Caille owner could remove the motor's sparkplug and screw the similarly threaded handle unit in its place. Caille was famous for putting priming cups on its motors' cylinders. A few squirts of gas are deposited in the little brass cup, the valve opened for allowing the fuel directly into the cylinder, and then closed so that starting would be surer.

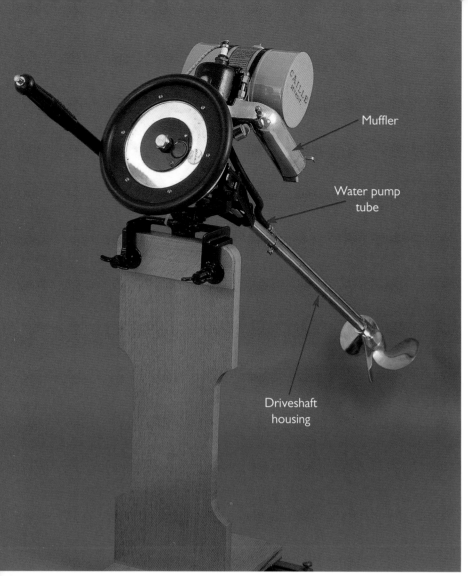

Muffler

Water pump tube

Driveshaft housing

Brand Name: Caille
Model: LD 21
Serial Number: 35411
Year of Manufacture: 1921
Manufacturer: Caille Perfection Motor Company
Place of Manufacture: Detroit, Michigan
Type: Two-cycle, Water-cooled, Flywheel magneto
  ignition.
Number of Cylinders: 1
Bore X Stroke: 2.625" X 2.500"
HP @ RPM: 2 @ 700
Weight: 70 lbs.
Original Price: NA
Owner: Robert Skinner

Like other Caille Liberty Drives and the Strelinger motors before them, this 1921's lower unit and water pump hose could be quickly removed from the powerhead for easy portage and stowing. The mixing valve, priming cup (angled for easy use with the powerhead in operating position), and the grease cup at the head of the drive shaft housing are featured here. The protrusion on the grease cup can be rotated in to inject the lubricant.

The firm even jumped in with a Liberty Twin (opposed, port/starboard cylinders) for 1924 through 1927. These had two more horses than our subject engines. Writing in a 1967 *Antique Outboarder*, respected vintage motor restorer, Marcus Wright, described a Liberty Twin he'd put together from a pair of parts motors. "The [Caille] Liberty was very well built. Machining and castings were superior to that in many contemporary motors." It may be said that the company's expertise in manufacturing gaming machines that required a mechanically inviting quality was oft translated in its outboard products.

So why didn't Liberty Drive overtake conventional models? By the early 1920s, most outboard makers better read the marketplace and incorporated tilting as standard. Perhaps because most outboarding took place in water of at least a few feet deep, Liberty Drive's long protruding "lower unit" seemed like overkill. Maybe,

even in pre-litigious America, people recognized the danger of spinning, relatively distant, shallow water propeller blades. Wright notes a drawback quickly apparent to any Liberty Drive operator. "Steering is a bit clumsy as the steering handle is located only [about] 14 inches ahead of the [motor mount] pivot point, which [means that] the propeller is located 46 inches aft of the steering pivot point! It requires a lot of effort to return to a straight course after turning hard. When making a close turn, it was found easier to push down on the steering handle, thus lifting the propeller partly out of the water, reducing the turning effort. Remember, the propeller is nearly four feet behind the boat!" Wright then offered the opinion that this impacted Liberty Drive's public acceptance, as "no other contemporary engine seems nearly as hard to steer."

That unknown Caille executive's prediction of direct-drive outboard sovereignty didn't materialize. In fairness to the mode, though, it can best conventional rivals in shallow water, and has reemerged from time to time. Most notable defenders of this faith include the University of Minnesota's student engineering outboard motor projects called Gophers, the Gierholtt/Hess of the 1920s, a Palmer prototype, British ATCO's post-World War Two Boatimpellers, and Zündapp, which is covered later in this volume.

Setting a Standard for Speed and Performance

ELTO SPEEDSTER AND QUAD

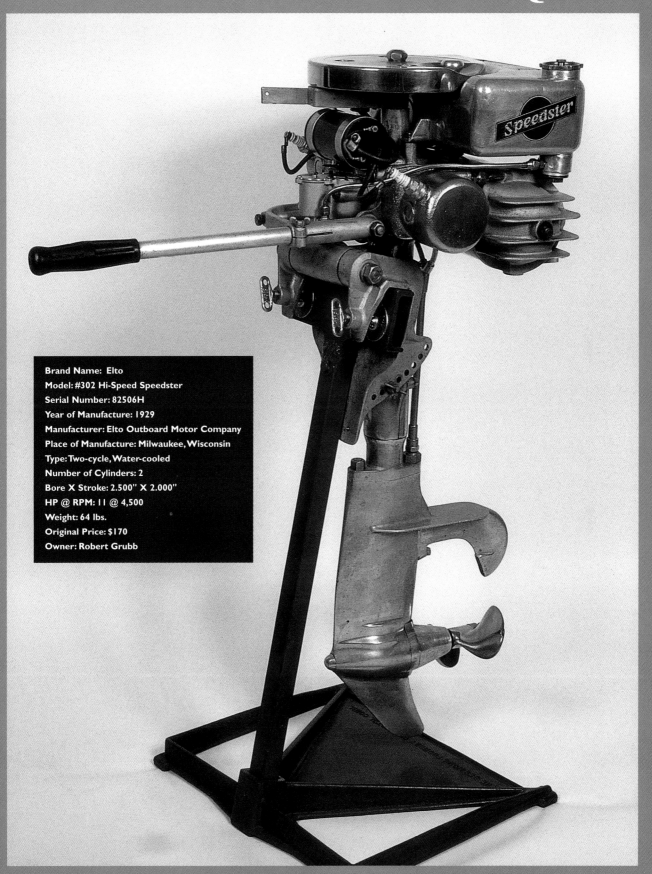

Brand Name: Elto
Model: #302 Hi-Speed Speedster
Serial Number: 82506H
Year of Manufacture: 1929
Manufacturer: Elto Outboard Motor Company
Place of Manufacture: Milwaukee, Wisconsin
Type: Two-cycle, Water-cooled
Number of Cylinders: 2
Bore X Stroke: 2.500" X 2.000"
HP @ RPM: 11 @ 4,500
Weight: 64 lbs.
Original Price: $170
Owner: Robert Grubb

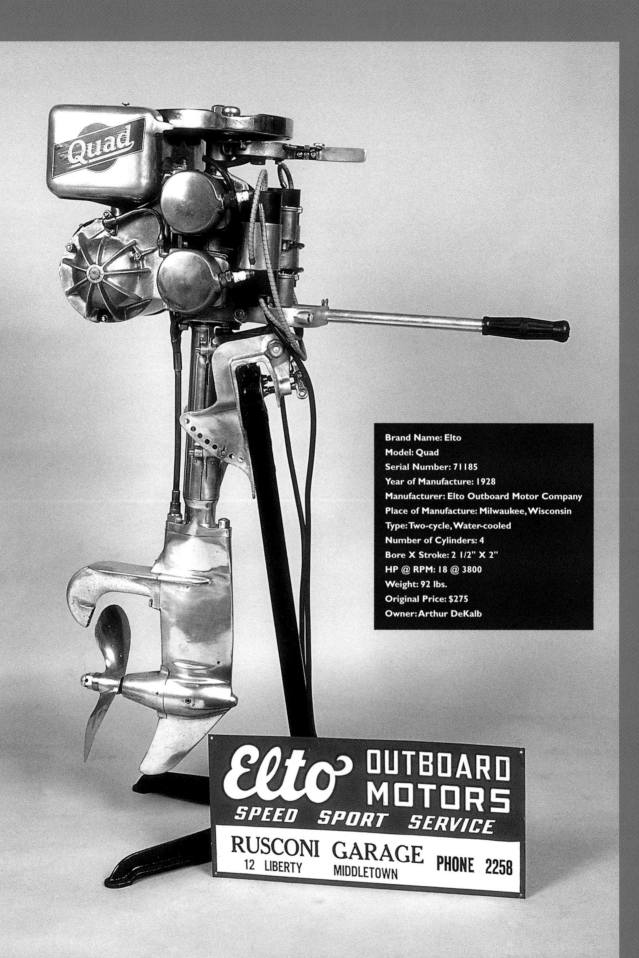

Brand Name: Elto
Model: Quad
Serial Number: 71185
Year of Manufacture: 1928
Manufacturer: Elto Outboard Motor Company
Place of Manufacture: Milwaukee, Wisconsin
Type: Two-cycle, Water-cooled
Number of Cylinders: 4
Bore X Stroke: 2 1/2" X 2"
HP @ RPM: 18 @ 3800
Weight: 92 lbs.
Original Price: $275
Owner: Arthur DeKalb

le Evinrude's covenant not to compete in the outboard industry ended by 1920. His cherished wife's health having improved during the hiatus, he returned to motor making with a flourish. But this new venture, begun in 1921, could not legally bear the Evinrude name, as this had been sold among the assets of his first outboard organization. Oddly, the successor Evinrude firm had no interest in Ole's 1918 idea to forgo a heavy cast iron, single-cylinder rowboat motor in favor of a lighter twin built largely of war-proved aluminum. So, free to tell the original Evinrude people to go fly a kite, he and Bess formed the Elto Outboard Motor Company and began making these light twins. In fact, the company's name, possessing the modern sounding ring of Kodak or Delco, got coined via Bess's doodling with the idea of an Evinrude-built light twin outboard — ELTO. A legal loophole allowed for each Elto identification plate to also include the comforting reality, "designed and built by Ole Evinrude," near the engine's model/serial designations. It was a gutsy move for the impeccably behaved Evinrude family, and it paid off handsomely.

From late 1921 through the early 1930s, Elto sold thousands of its rudder-steered twins (affectionately dubbed "Ruddertwin"). through several editions of three to four horsepower. Into 1927, it was Elto's only model. While its clothesline rope-controlled, sizeable rudder and knob starting made the Ruddertwin look anachronistic in the model's later years, a cleverly designed "Propello Pump" caught prop-generated water pressure in the rudder scoop, sending it, void of any actual pump parts, to cool the cylinders. Additionally, an Atwater-Kent battery ignition/timer system gave the early Eltos some of the easiest starting in the business. When all was right with the world, a simple quarter-turn bounce of the flywheel against compression would typically bring the motor to life. Some Elto owners would accessorize their engine by replacing the polished aluminum knuckle-buster with a rope sheave, but any outboarder truly at one with his or her Elto never dreamed of canceling the show of simply motioning the powerhead to song through a quick backhand. Suffice it to say, all was well at Elto during Ruddertwin's heyday.

In 1927, the founders' college age son started pestering them about not resting on fishing motor laurels.

Ralph Evinrude wanted his dad to revisit a trio of more powerful Eltos that the senior Mr. Evinrude had surreptitiously built in 1923. They were four-cylinder models just under 32 cubic inches of piston displacement, concocted by combining a pair of early 15.9 cube Ruddertwins. One of the experimental engines had been loaned to Elto's Seattle, Washington distributor who, in a 1926 race, bettered 23 mph. This was a notable achievement and helped Ralph Evinrude enlist his mother in moving Ole away from solely offering twin-cylinder products. Somewhere early in this process, the simple but effective nomenclature, "Quad," got attached to the project. In a 1968 *Antique Outboarder*, longtime Elto/Evinrude official, W. Jim Webb recalled what happened next. "The need for speed was now recognized, and at this opportune moment, Ralph [really] entered the picture. A sophomore at the University of Wisconsin, [he] said, 'We must have the [perfected production] Quad for 1928.' From the time school let out until the New York Boat

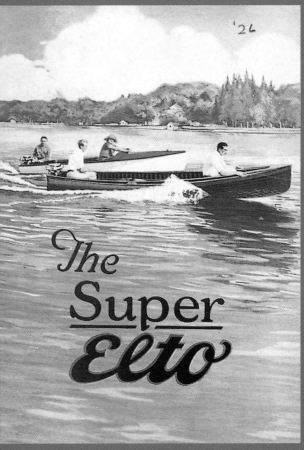

Prior to offering the 1928 Speedster or Quad, Elto built a solid reputation with its "Ruddertwin" model which was eventually dubbed "Super." By 1925, Ole Evinrude's second outboard company, Elto, began courting the fledgling outboard speed market. Three years later, Speedster and Quad truly put Elto on the "hot motor" map.

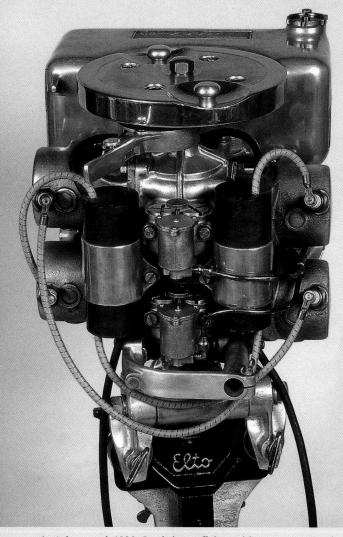

A nicely restored 1928 Quad shows-off the model's most interesting features: a double knuckle-buster flywheel, dual ignition coils (that get hooked to a six-volt battery), four individually cast cylinders, and dual poppet valve carburetors. A good battery ignition Elto and related Atwater Kent brand ignition system was an electro-mechanical engineering marvel. By simply rocking the flywheel (via the spring-loaded, pull up knuckle-buster knob) against compression stroke, the motor would bounce to life. The hole and wing nut arrangement on the Quad's (and Speedster's) steering yoke allows for most any length tiller arm to be used. In pre-steering wheel days, it wasn't uncommon for folks to use a piece of pipe long enough to facilitate mid-ship control. The timer "kill switch" button could be depressed until the motor just about stopped, then released to make the motor fire backwards for reverse operation. Very accomplished Elto operators could do this but some forgot that this made retarding the timer actually speed it up. The author once met a senior citizen who, as a youngster, had accidentally started a Quad backwards. One's natural inclination, when a motor kicks-up, is to push it back down. Over six decades later, the old-timer's hands were still scarred from the mishap.

Show in January, Ralph devoted all of his considerable energy to pushing the Quad and [two-cylinder] Speedster for the 1928 market. This pushing went on morning, noon, and night, seven days a week. Without it [Elto] wouldn't have had those motors ready and would have certainly missed a big part of the 1928 market."

Actually a half-Quad, trademarked "Speedster" was readied by September 1927. It was really a souped-up Ruddertwin, the perennial favorite that had been enlarged to 19.7 cubic inches of piston displacement

the previous year. The Speedster wore a finely streamlined lower unit that made nearly all competitors look downright clunky. This milestone motor might be compared to the original Ford Mustang. It was not terribly expensive and could be appreciated as a utilitarian, G-rated "family" item. But, like the original Mustang, the Speedster possessed sporty sex appeal that sent everyone from old anglers to youthful daredevils in beelines to local Elto dealers.

Part of the mystique was an exam that each debut edition Speedster sold had passed with flying colors. Webb recounted that either he or Ralph Evinrude "personally gave a final boat test to every one of the first 1,200 Speedsters produced in the fall of 1927. Every one of those first Speedsters had to check 22.5 miles per hour by stop watch timing over an accurate course on the upper Milwaukee River or it was sent back [to the plant for rebuilding.] Several times a day, we would rush up to the river test spot just above [Milwaukee's] North Avenue Bridge, test a load of motors, rush back to the office, and wait for the next call. Either one or the other of us was at the river most of the day."

Elto rivals must have figured that Speedster represented the firm's big gun for 1928. They weren't happy, but prepared to cope. Meantime, a few key Elto staffers were readying to produce parts like a bigger (than the Speedster's) fuel tank, dual knuckle-buster bedecked flywheel and a crankcase designed to accommodate two Speedster carbs, plus four Speedster cylinders, totaling 39.2 cubes. Prototypes of this Quad were considered too secret for downtown riparian spectators to catch with the naked eye, or through binoculars by a Caille, original Evinrude Company, or Johnson spy. Consequently, Quad tryouts took place in front of Ole and Bess's summer camp at Oconomowoc Lake, well past Labor Day (October through most of December until ice formed) and after it was rather certain no one was in earshot. So, it came as a real shock to competitors and a delightful surprise for outboard shoppers when display Quads were unveiled in New York. As was the case for the Speedster, orders rolled in at an amazing pace, even by Bess Evinrude's standards.

But the family's original company had yet another owner, and he aimed to augment his investment by capturing the public's fancy through acquiring speed records. He did so with the formidable 1928 Evinrude

Speeditwin which even gave the better-endowed (30 for Speeditwin vs. Quad's 40 cubes) Quad a run for its money. Debut Quads like our subject motor utilized iron pistons on bronze connecting rods. To be sure, these were sturdy components, but in racing, no ounce of extraneous weight can be tolerated. Webb remembered that in early summer 1928, "the fine performance of the Evinrude Speeditwins forced [Elto] to make a mid-season change and come out with a Hi-Speed model which had aluminum pistons, aluminum rods, larger ports, larger carburetor openings, etc. From [a then quite respectable] 3,500 RPM, the Quad's [crankshaft] speed went up to 4,300 plus. [This facilitated] a new World Time Trial record of 41.748 MPH with a Quad."

Out of the Hi-Speed Quad project came a similar hop-up for Speedster. Casual observers couldn't tell the difference between a standard seven-horse Service Speedster and its faster 11-12 hp (depending on RPM) sister. Like Hi-Speed Quad's particulars, much of the change occurred behind the cosmetics. An unassuming letter "H" stamped after the serial number is the most obvious sign that one is in contact with a Hi-Speed model. Hidden behind the muffler can, is an auxiliary breather that kicks in at about 2,500 RPM. Once active, it required the operator to richen the fuel (on the carburetor needle valve's fuel-to-air ratio). RPM could rush to some 4,500 when all was in tune and on a boat light enough to allow the prop to really rev.

The 1928 Elto (standard) Service Quad is an uncommon engine today, and its smaller sister, Hi-Speed Speedster is downright rare. Some owners of the latter, have retrofitted their motors with standard Service Speedster (a much more plentiful antique outboard) rods and pistons. When examined electronically today, few of these critical components in the aluminum Hi-Speed series have survived without at least microscopic cracking. Understandably, Elto never figured buffs would be trying to run these machines in the next century. Instead, the Service Quad, Speedster, and Hi-Speed models were simply thought of by Ole, Bess, Ralph, and associates as steps towards even faster, more dependable outboard motors. In the process, these important 1928 and 1929 developments would even help the family reclaim their old company.

Advanced Motors for 1929

That Beautiful Red Head

CAILLE MODEL 15

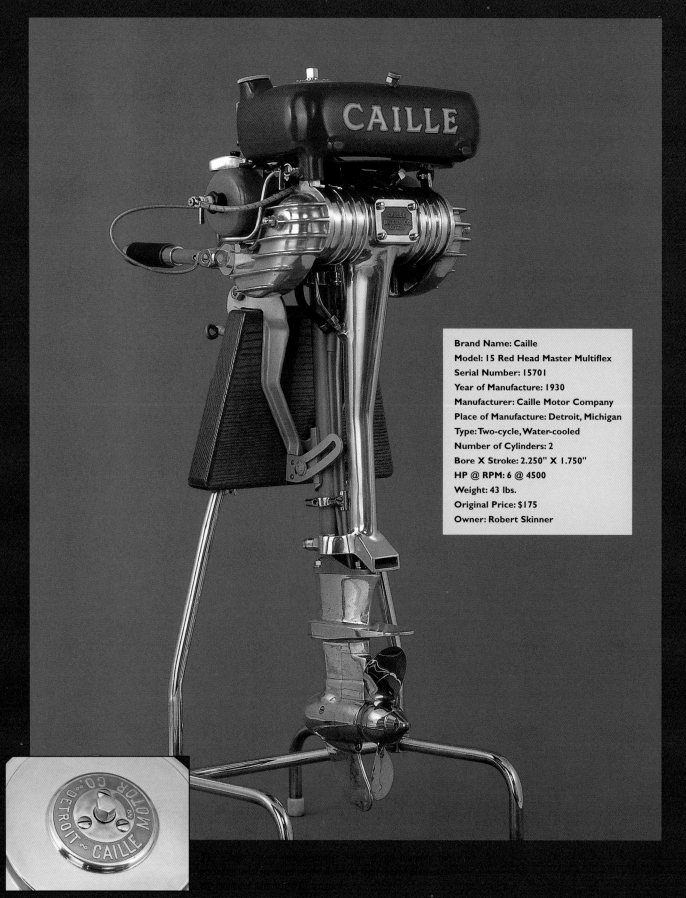

Brand Name: Caille
Model: 15 Red Head Master Multiflex
Serial Number: 15701
Year of Manufacture: 1930
Manufacturer: Caille Motor Company
Place of Manufacture: Detroit, Michigan
Type: Two-cycle, Water-cooled
Number of Cylinders: 2
Bore X Stroke: 2.250" X 1.750"
HP @ RPM: 6 @ 4500
Weight: 43 lbs.
Original Price: $175
Owner: Robert Skinner

Caille featured locks in its outboard advertising. It called this piece: "Protection against theft of your Caille outboard," and considered it an "insurance plan [that was] positive, yet inexpensive." While simple, the Caille's transom clamps, and their matching lock, were unique enough to warrant filing for a patent.

Nobody in the motor game really knew what 1930 would bring. Caille had just weathered some pretty hefty 1929 competition from the likes of Elto, Evinrude, and Johnson, but was still considered by outboard buffs to be a major player. Arguably, its line of 1930 models would be the company's most eye-catching ever. Racing motors from Caille were interesting, each fitted with a prop-in-front "tractor" lower gearcase. Few of them, though, wrested many kudos from the aforementioned brands. Most average outboard buyers flocked to the bigger makers or to the ubiquitous stables of budget models offered by Sears and Montgomery-Ward. That left Caille reaching for market share in a niche in which customers would appreciate the company's attention to quality, detail, and elaborate features such as the 5-Speed propeller. Selecting an electric start option on a variable-prop model really made the best-dressed list. While not necessarily more expensive than the rest, Caille outboards of this period had developed a kind of posh image. Advertising in upscale publications such as *National Geographic* seemed to imply that Caille motors were particularly built for those who could tell a fine outboard from an ordinary one. A 1930 Caille would more likely be noted dockside at a stately, three-storied New York Adirondack lodge than on the questionable stern of some old riverbank rowboat. Let someone representing the unwashed masses throw a plane-Jane Evinrude single on that old tub!

The Caille Model 15 shown here would look fine as a rich kid's first motor on a nicely varnished 12-foot

hull. Bright crimson paint on its fuel tank allowed the mill to be classified as a Red Head, the prominent trademark of every Caille, except the Liberty Single, in its 1930 series. The distinctive coloration had been the glory of the distinctive 1929 Lockwood brand Racing Chief, but Caille co-opted red for the value of quick mnemonic recognition. Further status was granted to the motor by Caille's addition of pleasingly vague model names. Like the string of identities borne by Royals, or the comforting "XL," "LE," "GT," et al now emblazoned on fancy cars, Cailles such as the Model 15 Red Head, were also knighted "Master" and "Multiflex." The latter was a trademarked description of the twist-grip control that facilitated carburetor butterfly valve motion, propeller feathering and steering. The company stubbornly held to the notion that a stationary powerhead and lower unit-only steering was the primary path to vibration-free outboard tillering for vertical shaft motors. Though this was a correct assumption with low-horsepower models, even the Model 15's six hp could put up a good torque vs. steering arm fight at full throttle. With no powerhead as ballast, it was just the driver (and possibly a factory installed spring) against the prop force. Through changes in carburetion bearings, and the adoption of an aluminum piston, Caille jumped the model 15's horsepower to eight in 1931 and again in 1932 (to 10 hp).

When the 1930 model year ended, the Great Depression had really begun accelerating. Stiff upper lips launched a very similar 1931 Caille line. By 1932, the red fuel tanks were still present, but the upscale Red Head theme was deemphasized. Instead, the company's promotional literature began tagging model numbers to bargain prices. The 1932 four-horse Model 79 for $79 serves as example. From 1933 through 1935, Caille tried to put a happy face on offering predominantly leftovers and price specials. Internally, motors from Elto, Evinrude, and Johnson had been somewhat more advanced than Caille's 1930 Red Head Series. Within a few years, the Detroit manufacturer's outboards were in need of redesign. Instead, Caille suspended production around late 1935. It had been a good run, though, and the Model 15 was among the most beautiful players in the outboard game.

Money Isn't the Object, Speed Is

OMC SPEEDI-BEE AND ELTO #632 RACER

Brand Name: OMC
Model: #176 Speedi-Bee Racer
Serial Number: 0006
Year of Manufacture: 1930
Manufacturer: Outboard Motors Corporation
Place of Manufacture: Milwaukee, Wisconsin
Type: Two-cycle, Water-cooled, Battery ignition
Number of Cylinders: 2
Bore X Stroke: 2.375" X 2.250"
HP @ RPM: 20 @ 6000
Weight: 115
Original Price: $400
Owner: Robert Skinner

Not even an economic depression took the smile off of Ole Evinrude's face in 1930. That year, he and his family became stockholders in three outboard makers besides Elto. Steve Briggs of the Briggs & Stratton small engine manufacturer had purchased Ole's original company in 1928 and envisaged forming a General Motors type of conglomerate for outboard production. He acquired Jackson, Michigan-based Lockwood as kind of a Pontiac to his new Evinrude Cadillac, but coveted the Chevy-esque innovation and sales volume enjoyed by Elto. When Ole, Bess, and Ralph wouldn't sell Elto outright, Briggs offered the family a way to reacquire their namesake firm. He formed a new outfit, Outboard Motors Corporation, with the Evinrudes, each holding executive powers in OMC, Evinrude, Elto, and Lockwood. The four years dormant Koban name also came with the deal, but OMC. officials decided to keep it retired.

The first true OMC-edition motor was a specialized mill that none of the partners believed would sell well. In fact only 25 of the Model #176 Speedi-Bee Racers were built. At $400 apiece, Speedi-Bee (sometimes noted in OMC documents as "Speedy-Bee") was produced to serve as a public relations tool. Not only would the concept outboard draw attention as one of the most advanced and aggressive of 1930, its performance was hoped to confirm the collective engineering talent assembled in the OMC amalgamation. Among the high-level technicians transferred to Ole's research and development shop was Lockwood's Fin T. Irgens. A brilliant outboard designer, "Irgy" had been responsible for Lockwood's 1929 Racing Chief, and was working on its anticipated 1930 successor, the Racing-Bee, when merger mania hit his company. With the conquest came Lockwood's R&D documents, ideas, and prototypes for the likes of a Flying-Four (cylinder) Lockwood as well as the updated Class "B" (approximately 20 cubic inches of piston displacement) racer. Irgens's new employers enthusiastically suggested he develop the latter into an OMC-branded engine. Our 1930 subject motor is one of the few survivors of that notable project. It is also represents the

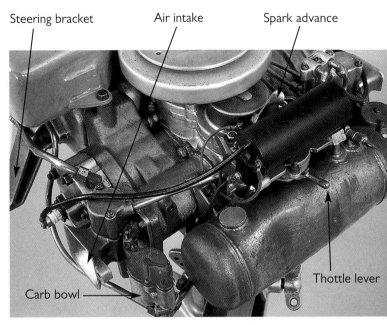

Steering bracket   Air intake   Spark advance

Carb bowl   Thottle lever

Throttle linkage is just above the Speedi-Bee's oil tank. The timer lever is right behind the ignition coil.

first production outboard to generate one horsepower per cubic inch, a feat that wasn't officially repeated until The National Pressure Cooker Company's Martin Division introduced the 20 cube, 20 horse model "200" well over two decades later.

Outboards like the Speedi-Bee and the soon-to-be mentioned Elto 632 were of such limited production that they went largely uncataloged. As a result, very little original documentation exists about these racers. When written down, the information seldom made it into a colorful brochure or owner's manual. Instead, a typewritten page or two of technical instructions might be shipped with the motor. The manufacturer figured that buyers of high performance mills would be refining their purchase on a race by race basis. This motivated motor makers to share the utmost engineering detail with the purchaser and, through follow-ups and feedback, represented economical R&D, but necessitated the voiding of any warranty. It is fortunate that three descriptive pages survived with our subject Speedi-Bee. The language is pure engineering department lingo, but is included here to transmit the flavor of Speedi-Bee's complexity.

"The crankshaft is permanently assembled with connecting rods, and roller bearings in place. It is drilled for oiling of the crankpin bearings, the oil being forced by a double gear pump to each Journal Bearing, and from the Journal Bearing to the crank pin bearing.

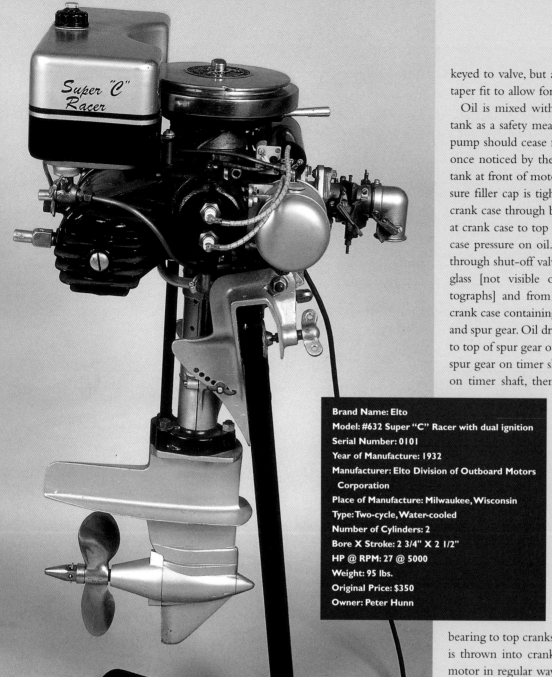

Super "C"
Racer

Brand Name: Elto
Model: #632 Super "C" Racer with dual ignition
Serial Number: 0101
Year of Manufacture: 1932
Manufacturer: Elto Division of Outboard Motors Corporation
Place of Manufacture: Milwaukee, Wisconsin
Type: Two-cycle, Water-cooled
Number of Cylinders: 2
Bore X Stroke: 2 3/4" X 2 1/2"
HP @ RPM: 27 @ 5000
Weight: 95 lbs.
Original Price: $350
Owner: Peter Hunn

keyed to valve, but are held in position on a taper fit to allow for final adjustments.

Oil is mixed with the gasoline in the gas tank as a safety measure only, in case the oil pump should cease functioning and is not at once noticed by the driver. Oil is put in oil tank at front of motor, which is air tight. (Be sure filler cap is tight.) One pipe leads from crank case through ball check valve in elbow at crank case to top of oil tank putting crank case pressure on oil. Oil is led from oil tank through shut-off valve to left hand sight feed glass [not visible on motor in our photographs] and from there to upper part of crank case containing crank shaft ball bearing and spur gear. Oil drains through ball bearing to top of spur gear on crank shaft and then to spur gear on timer shaft, then to ball bearing on timer shaft, then to bevel gears driving rotary valves, lubricating bottom bearing on timer shaft and is finally caught by double gear oil pump and faced by one set of gears through bottom journal bearing to lower crank shaft pin bearing and by other set of gears to right hand sight feed glass, and from here through top journal sealing bearing to top crankshaft pin and then the oil is thrown into crank case and passes out of motor in regular way after lubricating rotary valves and pistons. When the motor is running there is a solid flow of oil through the left hand sight feed glass and a spray of oil through the right sight feed glass.

Due to the high speed of the motor [up to 6500 RPM], a solid steel flywheel is used on crankshaft and instead of high tension magneto, a closed circuit battery ignition is employed. The leads from the battery are connected through a switch to the coil and ground connections. The timer is mounted on top of crank case at front of flywheel. Due to the closed circuit type of ignition, the [6 volt Hot Shot] battery is short lived and should be renewed often to assure a hot spark at all times.

Two float feed carburetors are used, one on each side of the motor in line with the rotary valves. Mixture is regulated by needle valve adjustment and controlled by barrel valves in carburetor bodies

Two rotary valves are driven in opposite directions by bevel gears from a vertical timer shaft. The timer shaft is driven at crankshaft speed by a steel spur gear on the crankshaft. The timer shaft drives a closed circuit timer mechanism on top of the crank case. If the motor is disassembled to correctly act the rotary valves, proceed as follows: Replace the cylinders leaving off the cylinder heads and put timer shaft in place in accordance with marking on spur gear on timer shaft and crankshaft. Turn crankshaft in running direction (clockwise) until pistons just close by-pass port, then insert rotary valves in chambers in such position that carburetor intake side of rotary valve just starts to open. CAUTION — Be sure to determine in which direction rotary valves revolve with crankshaft revolving clockwise. Bevel gears on rotary valves are not

attached to ends of rotary valve chambers. Barrel valves are inter-connected by means of central throttle and choke levers. Throttle is operated by Bowden wire control. Be sure that when throttle lever is in open position that both barrel valves are wide open. These can be inspected by removing carburetor and spark plug hoods which should be left attached at all times. A spring return to the closed position on throttle control at forward end of boat is recommended to prevent water from entering motor in case of a tip over.

Water cooling is accomplished by a forward direction scoop on the gear housing and the motor must not be operated at low boat speeds as overheating will result. Muffler is water cooled, water leaving muffler at rear.

Each motor is given individual [factory] attention in machining, assembling and testing and is required to show adequate performance on a dynamometer before release for shipment."

Even in a 1930 economy, Speedi-Bee's significant $400 sticker couldn't really cover the cost of hand-crafting such an engine. Major outboard makers were spending a ton of cash on racing endeavors. As the economic Depression intensified, none really could spare these funds. Actually, by 1932, it was only OMC interests battling Johnson on the racecourse. Caille had essentially dropped out of the contest. Meantime, OMC's Speedi-Bee was deemed too costly to continue manufacturing, especially by hand, and was discontinued after 25 engines. That left Johnson's model

"SR" as the "B" Class standard. OMC offered Class "C" (30 cubic inch) drivers its Elto Super "C" and Evinrude Speeditwin Racers to battle Johnson's model "PR." Here, the Elto #632 accessorized the line with a dual ignition feature. While young buffs must have theorized that two sparkplugs in each cylinder made the #632 faster than the "regular," albeit far from ordinary, model, #631 standard ignition Super "C" Racer, the extra plugs only provided backup in the event a sister plug failed due to a problem wire, electrode, cracked insulator, or oil fouling. There were some unscrupulous racers who tried disabling opponents' motors by knocking into their sparkplugs with the pointy boat bows. Perhaps the additional plug on a #632 came in handy there, too.

Our #632 has a solid steel flywheel, battery ignition, sleek Elto racing lower unit, and oil tank like its predecessor, the Speedi-Bee, but its single carb and less complicated internal rotary valve fuel induction system allowed it to be built more cost effectively than the 10 cubic inch (of piston displacement) smaller Speedi-Bee. Incidentally, the steel flywheel was in response to the higher (4000+) RPM. Many an early aluminum flywheel was known to begin disintegrating at such speeds. The featured Dual Ignition Super "C" Racer was discovered in nearly useless condition peeking through a pile of obsolete racing motors and parts. Actually, much of it had been cannibalized decades before. Only the bare bones powerhead and one dual ignition cylinder remained. Elto restorer Sam Vance recognized the rare 632 identification tag amidst all the grime, rescued the vintage racer, and then set out collecting and fabricating parts for its revitalization. Although Ole Evinrude passed away only two years after #632 - 0101 left his factory, no doubt there'd be a smile if he were to see the Elto and Speedi-Bee still ready to race today.

Solid steel flywheel

Spark advance lever

Twin spark plugs

Oil tank   Air intake   Coil

Oil from the front-mounted tank is fed directly to this Elto #632 Super "C" Racer's main bearings. Dual plugs in each cylinder didn't make the motor go faster than just one in each, but sure came in handy if one got cracked or oil-fouled. The inverted air intake on the single Tillotson carburetor is so positioned to eliminate the chance of dowsing the fuel passages with water. Like all Eltos of the 1920s and early 1930s, this one has battery ignition that used a six-volt Eveready "Hot Shot."

JOHNSON K-65 ALTERNATE FIRING TWIN

Sight glass
fuel gauge

Kill switch

Carburetor

Air intake

Note the "sight glass" fuel gauge on tank. This model's simple, but effective carburetor is a direct descendant of the one employed on Johnson's first motor, the Light Twin/Water Bug. Finn Irgens, the talented engineer who designed OMC's Speedi-Bee had helped concoct the Johnson carb when working with the Johnson brothers around 1921.

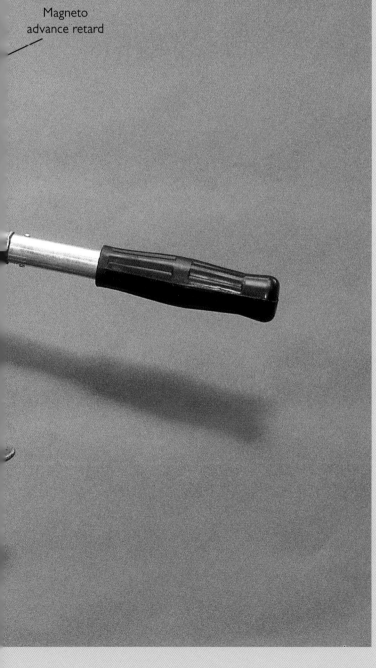

Brand Name: Johnson
Model: K-65
Serial Number: 200535
Year of Manufacture: 1933
Manufacturer: Johnson Motor Company
Place of Manufacture: Waukegan, Illinois
Type: Two-cycle, Water-cooled
Number of Cylinders: 2
Bore X Stroke: 2-1/8" X 1-31/32"
HP @ RPM: 9.2 @ 4000
Weight: 63 lbs.
Original Price: $144.50
Owner: Arthur DeKalb

Magneto
advance retard

A rumor circulated through the early-to-mid-1930s outboard community that Evinrude was secretly keeping rival Johnson afloat. While it certainly seemed like a ludicrous idea that a struggling front-runner would care to aid its only formidable competitor, there was actually little madness in such a method. Though making some of the world's most innovative and dependable outboard motors, Johnson had simply lost its way on the rough roads of a darkening economy. What it needed was the disciplined business detail of a Bess Evinrude and loyal associates. What it got was a series of bank-appointed receivers counting the days until a better assignment arrived. Production numbers began a period of rather wild fluctuation, from 24,776 motors serialized in 1930, down to 8,548 the following year, just 6,103 for 1932, a go-for-broke 41,152 in 1933 when the pictured K-65 came off the line — then dropped to 10, 787 Sea Horses during the 1934 model year. Reportedly, there were still leftovers from previous production runs.

Though acceptable volume for the times, Johnson's high corporate operational costs gulped profits. Consumers, increasingly impecunious, still maintained high regard for the company's Sea Horse outboards, even if they could only dream of affording one. Few probably realized that Johnson had declared bankruptcy in 1932. Meantime, the fiscally conservative Outboard Motors Corporation kept pinching pennies. Its excess never imagined building a sprawling plant like the state-of-the-art, lakeside Johnson factory at Waukegan, Illinois. Their parsimony readied them for rainy days. As Johnson debuted the 1933 line, Evinrude especially admired their competitor's smooth running twins like the alternate-firing model K-65. Evinrude knew that the widest outboard market rested in the utilitarian, family fishing motor domain. They also had an understanding of how the Sea Horse line could be maximized by focusing on basics.

Johnson's first decade had been anything but simple. In meteoric fashion rivaling late 1990s dot.com internet startups, the Johnson Motor Company burst onto the 1922 outboard season with a 35-pound opposed twin that, even today, is considered by buffs to be a fine performer. Coincidentally given the same "Light Twin" designation as Ole's newly-introduced

speed engineering. By 1926, they had truly captured boating attention with the offering of their model P-30, six-horse "Big Twin" that could hit 23+ mph on a light hull. At that time, such a clip was considered revolutionary. Their fame grew, causing their big engines to get even bigger. For 1928, the old Johnson South Bend, Indiana plant was replaced with a larger one in Waukegan, Illinois. Even Ole's people considered it to be the world's finest outboard factory. For good measure, another was opened in Ontario, Canada.

Elto, the two-horse Johnson (also called "Waterbug") quickly captured a significant chunk of the growing outboard market, and probably caused the era's Elto Light Twin to be re-dubbed "Ruddertwin." While, through about 1927, Ole's group stayed happy with one basic model, the Johnson family and associates felt the urge to quickly branch out, adding motors small and large to its catalogs. Much of the growth stemmed from the introduction of high-performance models that fed the Johnson brothers' (Lou, Harry, Clarence, and bother-in-law, Warren Conover) penchant for

The 1929 Johnsons were the first to wear a Sea Horse logo. The biggest Sea Horse featured the brothers' unique, gear-driven, external rotary valve fuel induction system, and four cylinders. During a test of a compression release for easier rope starting, in which a bank of two cylinders was relieved of cranking air pressure, the experimenting siblings noticed how silkily their big Sea Horse 26 would run on a single bank of alternately firing cylinders. Figuring results would be even better if the other pair of pistons (that were only adding drag in a non-compression mode) were eliminated, the R&D crew built up a powerhead with two, rear-pointing cylinders. The outcome pleased the Johnson fellows and became the model K-50 in 1930. Under various model designations and with several styling updates, this motor was a Johnson star for nearly two decades. Our 1933 subject K-65 presents a nice picture of the alternate firing K's early form. About three years later, when Evinrude interests stepped in to buy Johnson (for less than what the Waukegan plant had cost), the model K's solid reputation was considered to be among the firm's finest assets.

Over the years, Johnson had several depictions of the critters representing their Sea Horse trademark. The "angry dragon" style on this model K-65 was employed from 1929 through much of the 1930s. The alternate firing K remained in the catalog — with various updates — through 1948. A rear view best shows decal detail, the exhaust cutout (in open position to add a bit of extra zip to output), and the in-line, alternate firing cylinder assembly with sparkplugs.

Few Parts, Few Pounds, and Cute as the Dickens!

CLARKE TROLLER

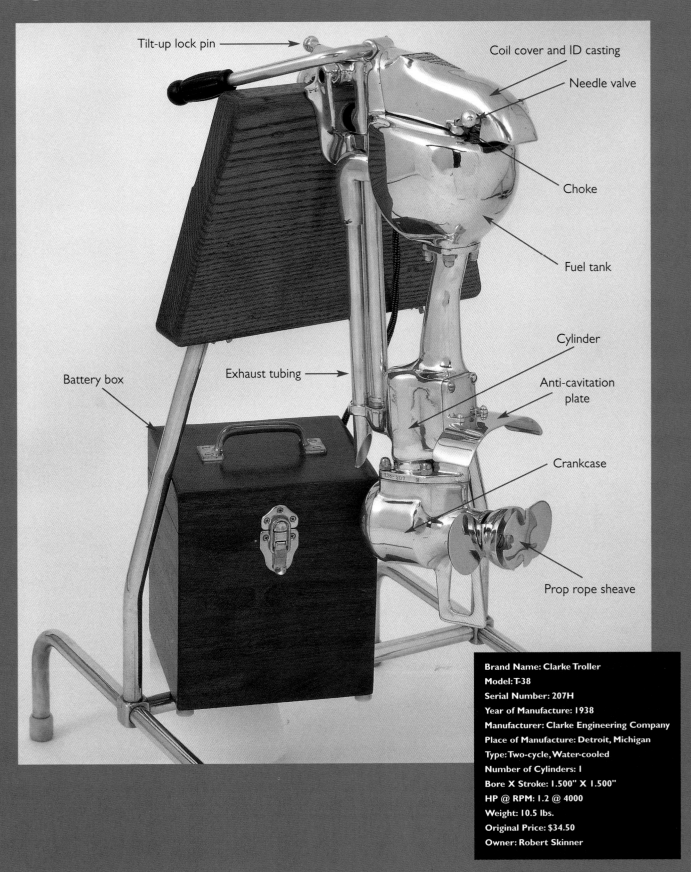

Tilt-up lock pin

Coil cover and ID casting

Needle valve

Choke

Fuel tank

Cylinder

Anti-cavitation plate

Crankcase

Prop rope sheave

Battery box

Exhaust tubing

Brand Name: Clarke Troller
Model: T-38
Serial Number: 207H
Year of Manufacture: 1938
Manufacturer: Clarke Engineering Company
Place of Manufacture: Detroit, Michigan
Type: Two-cycle, Water-cooled
Number of Cylinders: 1
Bore X Stroke: 1.500" X 1.500"
HP @ RPM: 1.2 @ 4000
Weight: 10.5 lbs.
Original Price: $34.50
Owner: Robert Skinner

The Detroit-based Clarke Engineering firm's airplane circled a Florida field then gently bounced to its landing. There to take possession of the craft's unique cargo was C. A. Pound, president of Gainesville's Baird Hardware Company. As the cabin door swung open, a smiling fellow handed Pound a tiny, silver outboard motor. After being the subject of a few "grin and grab" publicity photos, the miniscule kicker was touted as the factory's debut Clarke Troller. It then went on sale at Pound's store.

That happy stunt took place in late 1937 when even the most compact outboards weighed about 20 pounds and could get mighty hot and greasy during operation. The new Clarke product barely weighed in at half that figure, wouldn't be hot to the touch, and didn't seem to be subject to accumulation of oily dirt. Plus, it remained cleanly without a flywheel, water pump, driveshaft, gears, water pipes, fuel lines, or spark control. Clarke's big roll-out ad in the December 1937 *Motor Boating* depicted the engine next to a truncated yardstick. "Only 21 inches over all," the copy bragged. "World's lightest practical outboard motor. Entirely new principle . . . radically new and different." Frankly, the ad did such a good job outlining the Troller's uniqueness that its points are included herein:

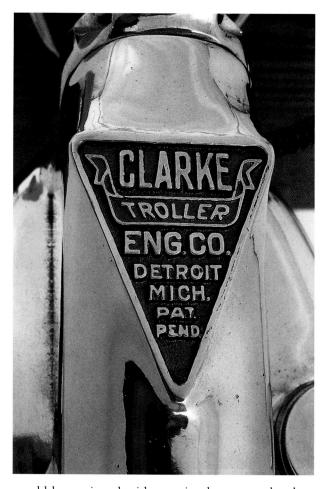

> "Cooled by direct submersion [powerhead rides underwater and prop is at end of crankshaft]. Carburetor and ignition mechanism enclosed (sic) in metal housing make motor waterproof, rainproof, and sprayproof. Can be carried with full tank of gasoline. Low center of gravity — below waterline — actually contributes to stability. It is ideal for canoe as well as boat use. Uses automobile type battery ignition . . . light dry cell providing current for ignition as well as for legally required light. Clean! And stays that way, with its polished aluminum finish. Smooth, streamlined exterior without dirt-catching projections or greasy parts, allowing it to be handled freely without soiling hands or clothing. Easy to carry anywhere — stores in small space — economical to operate. Just the motor for fishing or cruising. Powerful — developing 1.2 horsepower. Economical — operates approximately 1-1/2 hours on a quart [as opposed to other makers' "hours-per-gallon" rating] of fuel."

Toronto, Canada resident D.R. Clarke had come up with an attractive little package, indeed. When (in the King's English) fully "kitted-out," one's Clarke Troller would be equipped with carrying bag, canoe bracket, and clock spring "chicken starter." Getting the model airplane size motor going provided interesting pageantry. Once secured to a craft, the Troller is locked (with a spring loaded pin) in an approximately 40 degee from the water surface tilt. With the battery connected to related ignition wires down to the tiny model airplane "V" sparkplug, and a small choke lever depressed, the Clarke operator wraps a starter rope around the sheave on the propeller hub then gives a pull. The "chicken starter" wand could also be used to spin the prop. Most models wore a brass, variable-pitch propeller. Adjustments were to be made prior to starting, by loosening inset Allen screws and feathering each blade as desired. Once a Clarke came to life, it usually wouldn't run long unless very gingerly tilted back down into the water. Here, aggressive prop pitch almost never worked to advantage. Just over three miles per hour is considered a near record Clarke speed. Its 4000 RPM rating appears to include 25 percent hyperbole.

There appear to be many obvious and some nuance variations over the company's 1938-1941 run. For example, a two-piece fuel tank was introduced around late 1939, some motors were of a magnesium alloy, some others were painted silver instead of polished. An extended length model became available, as did a twin-cylinder version of 19.5 pounds and three horses. By this time, Clarke boosted the advertised output of its single to 1.3 (instead of 1.2) hp. It's not certain how many Clarke Trollers were actually built, but it's safe to say many survived. The author once served as the Antique Outboard Motor Club special interest registrar for Clarke motors. As of 2001, some 200 Clarkes made the list. Undoubtedly, more are out there, as they have a knack for conveniently hiding in very small places.

The sub-compact design presented some excellent outboard possibilities. In reality, however, probably only a devoted vintage outboard hobbyist would have the patience to enjoy tangling with one of these temperamental kickers on a boat. It is the author's theory that most every Clarke discovered looks to be in great shape because few were run enough to incur much wear or many tankfulls of oily gas. Early retirement on a garage rafter was the lot of many persnickety Clarkes. They were simply too cute to discard, though for many years only the most sentimental boat shop proprietor would even take the things as $5 trade-in credit. No matter, there are likely hundreds of collectors today who'd probably charter a plane to go get one.

A postscript to this narrative is in order, as a small model engineering firm introduced a 1/3 scale Clarke single in 2000 and a twin-cylinder version for 2001. The glowplug-based (as opposed to spark-based) models became an instant hit with the miniature engine crowd and ironically make the original seem huge.

The official Clarke accessory "chicken starter" wand is supposed to allow motor to be fired either in the water or while tilted. Its business end got wound like a watch. The Clarke operator would then mate the head to the prop's rope sheave, and spring loading would let go when the little lever near the handle was pushed. The canoe bracket was also a popular Clarke add-on for installation via bolts through the craft's gunwale.

THOR ALTERNATE 3

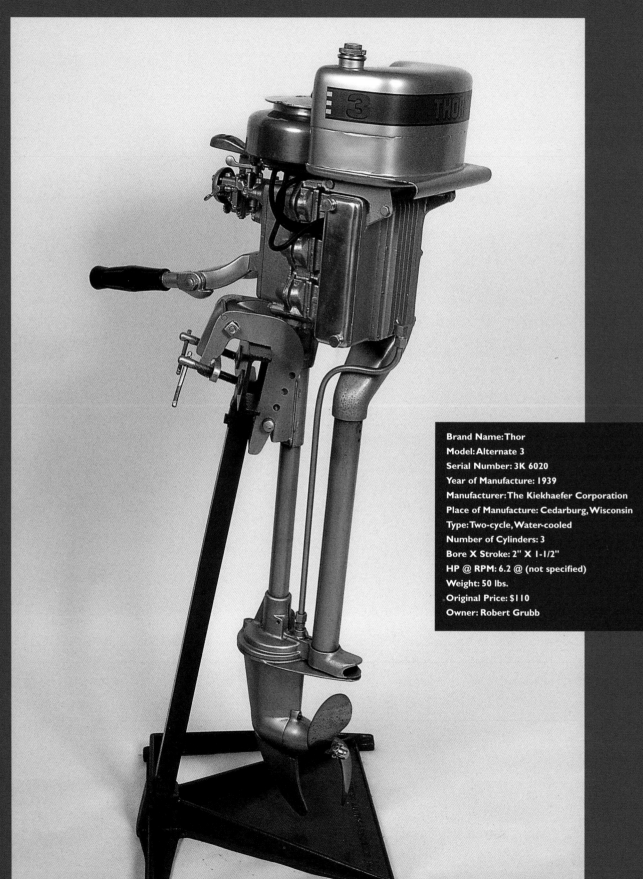

Brand Name: Thor
Model: Alternate 3
Serial Number: 3K 6020
Year of Manufacture: 1939
Manufacturer: The Kiekhaefer Corporation
Place of Manufacture: Cedarburg, Wisconsin
Type: Two-cycle, Water-cooled
Number of Cylinders: 3
Bore X Stroke: 2" X 1-1/2"
HP @ RPM: 6.2 @ (not specified)
Weight: 50 lbs.
Original Price: $110
Owner: Robert Grubb

Being first with an innovation doesn't always generate reward. Among other things, Thorwald Hansen pioneered alternate-firing, triple in-line cylinder outboard motor technology. Unfortunately, though, the motor's introduction did nothing to prevent Hansen's Cedarburg Manufacturing Company from sinking. During a slice of the 1930s, Hansen had enjoyed modest success making cheap, single-cylinder, Sea King outboards for catalog store Montgomery Ward, and selling some directly, under the Thor label, to small-time sporting goods dealers. Central to the motors' price advantage over competitors were inexpensive stampings of relatively mild steel that comprised critical components like the crankcase and lower unit casing. A basic and consequently temperamental mixing valve was responsible for metering fuel. Suffice it to say, not all of Hansen's bargain outboards started and ran the way their brochures promised. Once several thousand got into the hands of vacationers, more than a few of the optimistically-warranted (one year on anything caused by the maker) putt-putts were returned.

To add to his line, and quiet the growing criticism of the simplistic single, Hansen created an alternate-firing twin and the triple. They were named Pyramid 2 and Pyramid 3, even though such geometrical identification conjures thoughts of some sort of triangular arrangement, not a straight row. By their 1938 introduction, however, things at the indebted Wisconsin company were too out of shape for a white knight product debut rescue. Approximately 50 of the Pyramid twins and 20 triples got built. Some were still in the factory during early winter 1939 when E. Carl Kiekhaefer's group took possession of the comatose enterprise. A handful of these leftovers showed up in the nascent Kiekhaefer Corporation's April 1939 display at a Milwaukee outdoors show. Taking center stage, though, was a single-cylinder Streamliner model. However, Mr. Kiekhaefer is believed to have quickly understood that, in any denomination, the Thor designs offered limited potential.

Our subject engine, a 1939 model numbered 3K 6020, is the second to the last of 20 such triples assumed to have been assembled by Kiekhaefer, although it wears a plain flywheel-mounted rope sheave plate, not one that says Kiekhaefer Corporation.

It is not known for sure whether any of these later Thors resulted from renumbered 1938 versions. Kiekhaefer records note 100 alternate-firing twins for 1939, but indicate the discontinuance of opposed twins offered by Thor from 1936-1938.

Although gung-ho to transform the standard Thor single into a streamlined machine, Carl Kiekhaefer made no such cowling conversion for the alternate firing models. Some were treated to real carburetion (replacing Hansen's mixing valves) and all of the '39s got redubbed Alternate 2 or Alternate 3. The original Pyramid label made little sense to Kiekhaefer. What did seem right to the novice outboard magnate, however, was upgrading the triple's lower unit. As built by Hansen, the 6.2-hp motor had a steel stamped gearcase and light-duty gears better suited to a two-horse motor. Kiekhaefer determined to produce a conventional lower unit capable of handling these bigger engines. The featured Alternate 3 is one of only a very few Thor products to wear a cast-aluminum gearcase. Interestingly, however, another such motor has surfaced that was reported to be taken from the Thor factory prior to Kiekhaefer's arrival, suggesting Hansen had toyed with an aluminum lower end. Still, our subject triple motor could be considered a factory experimental version that was probably let go in the late fall of 1939 when Kiekhaefer's Thor dalliance shifted into the serious business of renovating his new Mercury outboard line. Imagination, determination, and a willingness to innovate, then move on, made for some exciting times ahead.

Thor single from which all other Thors were derived.

Kiekhaefer's Pollywog
THOR STREAMLINER

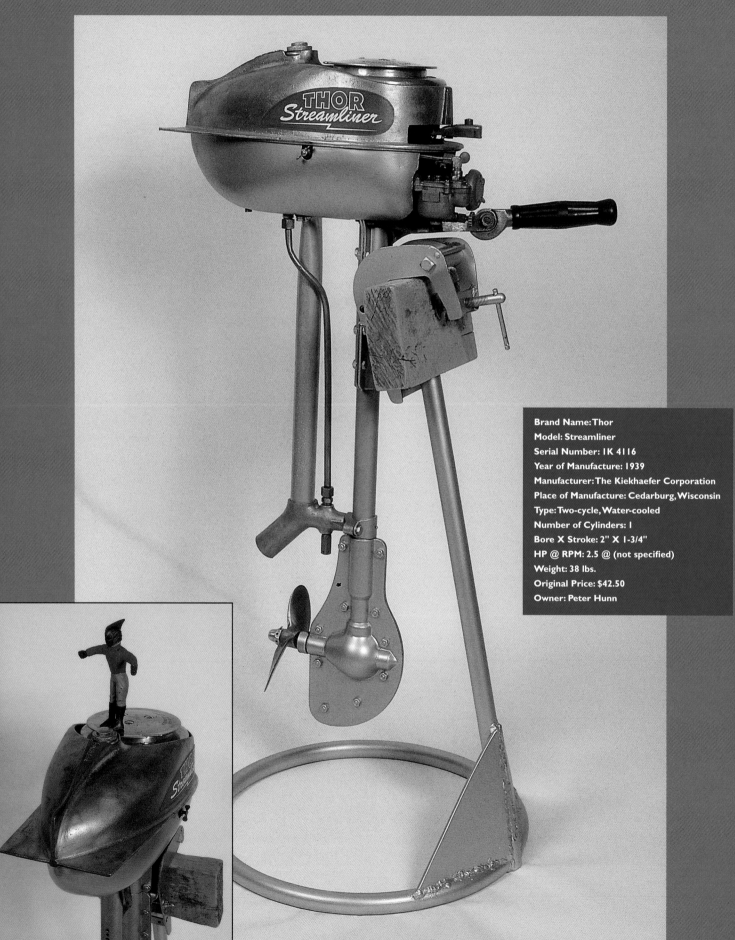

Brand Name: Thor
Model: Streamliner
Serial Number: IK 4116
Year of Manufacture: 1939
Manufacturer: The Kiekhaefer Corporation
Place of Manufacture: Cedarburg, Wisconsin
Type: Two-cycle, Water-cooled
Number of Cylinders: 1
Bore X Stroke: 2" X 1-3/4"
HP @ RPM: 2.5 @ (not specified)
Weight: 38 lbs.
Original Price: $42.50
Owner: Peter Hunn

Headquartered in Cedarburg, Wisconsin, the fledgling Kiekhaefer Corporation hoped to convince 1939 outboard buyers that it had a handle on modernity. Unfortunately, the firm had to quickly do so using components from its predecessor's noticeably unsophisticated Thor-brand inventory. This moribund marque was begun some six years earlier with, among a roster of other troublesome parts, steel stampings and crude mixing valves. Company co-founder, E. Carl Kiekhaefer ditched the simplistic fuel metering device in favor of carburetion from that genre's leader, Tillotson. Then he set about giving the now better-running Thor a contemporary look.

Kiekhaefer ordered that Thor's oft-dented, neckpillow-like gas tank be removed to make way for a cast aluminum, teardrop-shaped fuel compartment that would integrate a sleek covering for much of the funny little outboard's powerhead. Inspiration for the design can be seen in the era's aircraft, science fiction comic books and Saturday matinee spaceman serials. As a cloaking device for the rest of the lumpy old Thor identity, wraparound lower shrouds were also mandated. The resultant motor, dubbed *Streamliner*, went from concept to reality in about a fortnight.

Promoted as Kiekhaefer Corporation's star product, it was prominent in most every 1939 boating season ad the new company could afford. Enigmatically, though, less than 475 Thor Streamliners were built. It is not recalled whether this tiny production run stemmed from the motor's late (spring, rather than the previous fall) introduction, modest buyer response, or Carl Kiekhaefer's conviction that an outboard possessing any Thor trait had no long-term market potential. The author believes the latter. While Streamliner's top seemed futuristic, the model's lower unit exposed multiple lengths of plumbing that stuck out like a pretty ballerina on bulky wooden crutches. Once some of these motors hit dealer showrooms, Kiekhaefer lost little time in designing a completely new outboard worthy of his Streamliner moniker. Not only did the 1940 version sport a nicely cowled engine, but its lower unit exhibited the sveltest lines in the industry. To help

highlight this creation, the Thor label was instantly and quietly retired. Kiekhaefer's new motors, including a model that retained the Streamliner designation, would wear the Mercury banner.

The pictured Streamliner came to the author in trade for an Elto Quad ignition timer and some Indian Motorcycle Company outboard parts. Little is known about serial number 1K4116 Thor's adventures between its early spring 1939 birth to the aforementioned 1997 swap and subsequent revitalization. Avid antique outboard operators might be aghast to learn that, following its rebuild, the featured kicker spent several years in a bedroom wrapped in a blanket. Its removal to one of *Beautiful Outboards'* photo shoots prompted some strange glances by the author's wife who had thought the covering to simply be a spare quilt symmetrically rolled up for a sub-zero night.

Before its stealthy indoor life, no doubt the powerhead had seen a bit of backyard mechanic "monkeying," as some previous owner hacksawed away an inch or so of the front, top cowling in order to free this assembly from the stubbornly protruding spark advance lever. Apparently, other purchasers of the model independently discovered such a fix. Several Streamliners have surfaced with similar slices. Because the cuts appear horizontally longer on the "fast" side of the lever path, it may be that operators felt the cowl dimension prevented the spark advance from reaching the engine's full potential. After all, in the imaginations of boaters, the then-modern fuel tank/cowling design certainly made Streamliner look like it should step lively. Of course the mid-1930s Thor innards, to which it was still shackled, kept the results more focused on promise than speedy performance. Though originally a hurried attempt to concoct something useful and attractive from left over Thor standard singles, the Thor Streamliner is arguably the seminal link between 1930s fantasy and the technology associated with the modern Mercury line.

EVINRUDE MATE AND CUB

Brand Name: Elto
Model: #4264 Cub
Serial Number: 05546
Year of Manufacture: 1941
Manufacturer: Elto Motor Company
Place of Manufacture: Milwaukee, Wisconsin
Type: Two-cycle, Water-cooled
Number of Cylinders: 1
Bore X Stroke: 1-1/8" X 1"
HP @ RPM: 1/2 @ 4000
Weight: 8-1/2 lbs.
Original Price: $26.50
Owner: Robert Grubb

Brand Name: Evinrude
Model: #4263 Mate
Serial Number: 02603
Year of Manufacture: 1939
Manufacturer: Evinrude Motor Company
Place of Manufacture: Milwaukee, Wisconsin
Type: Two-cycle, Water-cooled
Number of Cylinders: 1
Bore X Stroke: 1-1/8" X 1"
HP @ RPM: 1/2 @ 4000 RPM
Weight: 10 lbs.
Original Price: $34.50
Owner: Robert Grubb

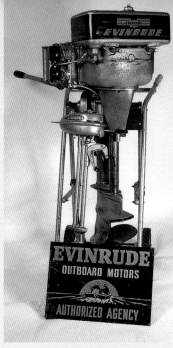

Something got the Evinrude/Elto group contemplating the development of a micropower outboard. Considering respectable travel time from idea to resulting good-to-go motor would take about a year, it's quite possible that Clarke Troller's 1938 fanfare served as catalyst. In any event, Evinrude and Elto each had a Lilliputian engine ready for the 1939 model year. The basic Elto Cub and deluxe Evinrude Mate were essentially identical products, except for powerhead cowling granted to the latter. This followed along with the business plan of what had become the Ralph Evinrude/Steve Briggs-operated Outboard Marine and Manufacturing Corporation. That is to say, Elto served as its economy line; Johnson the solid mainstay; and Evinrude represented the new technology and high-end quality brand. A similar positioning of Johnson and Evinrude was instituted in the late 1990s by the final incarnation of the successor Outboard Marine Corporation.

As a result of the Evinrude crown, the Mate was treated to some streamlined, teardrop-shroud styling. Still, both Mate and Cub hit the market shouting low prices. "A genuine Evinrude for only $34.50!" Mate ads announced. "Millions agree, it's boating's biggest buy! [and] It's a must with multitudes who can now enjoy a genuine Evinrude at everybody's price," were other promotional headlines. At less than 30 bucks, the Cub seemed even more remarkable to legions of water-loving youngsters who imagined a new outboard being finally within their fiscal reach. As both models aged, their prices dropped. The 1940-1941 Mate was reduced to $29.95, forcing the original 1939 $29.50 Cub sticker down to $26.50 for 1940-1941. Overruns of each were quietly offered in the 1942 catalogs and arguably could be had new, as leftovers or distributor/dealer "blow-outs" for around $25 and $20 respectively. A November

By 1942, Mate leftovers were still plentiful enough for the model's inclusion in the annual catalog. It received little editorial space, however, as Evinrude knew most outboard shoppers wanted a "real" motor, not the tiny 1/2-horse putt-putt. No matter, the 1942 line was cut short in March when production of civilian luxury items was halted due to war.

Vintage outboarding's most unlikely couple might be a giant Big Four together with the petite Mate. The Big Four is over 107 pounds heavier! The Evinrude sign hails from an era when both motors would be in showrooms.

1951 Evinrude-Elto service bulletin sent to dealers interested in suggested trade-in allowances, hedged on the diminutive duo's worth on the second-hand market and wouldn't even commit to a five-buck, ball-park figure.

It appears that more Cubs (about 6,000 made) than Mates (approximately 4,500) were produced. Most were built in 1939. In the era's cleaner vernacular, suffice it to say performance was not so hot, no matter the specific vintage. One would also be safe in indicating that the only folks taken in by such a small outboard were kids with imagination or bargain hunting adults lacking engine dynamics knowledge. Without meaning to be pejorative, the author believes women also fell victim to Mate and Cub's baby appearance and name brand clout. An old widower had tears in his eyes while recalling how his pretty wife took in sewing work and saved enough cookie jar money to finally be able to go to the local Evinrude dealer and pay cash for a cute little outboard she'd seen that past spring in a magazine. Though a dollar something short, the bride explained to the dealer's sympathetic spouse that the Cub was to be a Christmas present. It was under the tree a few days later. By a crackling holiday fireplace, the couple happily chatted about places the tiny Elto might take them during the next summer. "That darn thing never ran right," he smiled. "About, every fifth or sixth pull it'd pop a few times, though, and keep me trying. We ended up a long way from shore just on the motion from the starter rope spinning the flywheel and prop. My wife felt terrible about it, and wanted me to trade for a 'real' motor when we got some extra money. It's still clamped to a board on the side of my workbench. I hated that little Elto bugger for always making me row, but every time I look at it, I think of my dear wife's thoughtfulness."

Thinking of cost effectiveness, those who approved the half-horse project's final engineering drawings cut corners wherever possible. These measures called for a single crankcase/carburetor combo casting. Even so, the carb body was home to a goodly number of miniscule parts that were easily "boinged" into the drink if troubleshooting was tried on board. The owner of our topic engines noted in a 1982 *Antique Outboarder* that the real "weak point of [Mate and Cub] seems to be the [ignition] coils. [He] supposed their very small size coupled with the state of the art at the time [1939], led to poor durability. Starting the motors seems to be a bit irregular and chancy. You get a number of wraps of the starter cord around the small diameter rope sheave and give a good healthy yank. Whereupon the motor will likely spin down to a stop [its delicate carburetor poppet valve mocking all the while] After a couple of tries like this, it may suddenly start [with no warning and for little apparent reason over the previous attempt] and take off. These tiny motors generally do not idle great. Top speed is in the realm of a good electric trolling motor [about 3 mph]."

Upon cruising into a Geneva, New York marina in the late 1980s, the author bought a '39 Mate from the used motor rack. The storekeeper remembered it just hiding there between various bigger motors since the '50s. Amazingly, this gem still had spark and noticeable compression. Several hours of pulling, during each of three successive summers, though, never even made it burp. Comparatively, a slightly larger .9 horsepower Elto Pal in the author's collection feels as if it contains no compression and only intermittent spark. That 1937 engine will spring to life so quickly that it's as if the motor wants a boat ride as much as does captain and passengers. Considering a new 1937 Pal only cost three dollars more than a new 1939 Mate, it is quite realistic to assume that the Pal (with separately cast carb and crankcase, as well as bigger coil) is about as small a micro-horsepower outboard as is dependably practical.

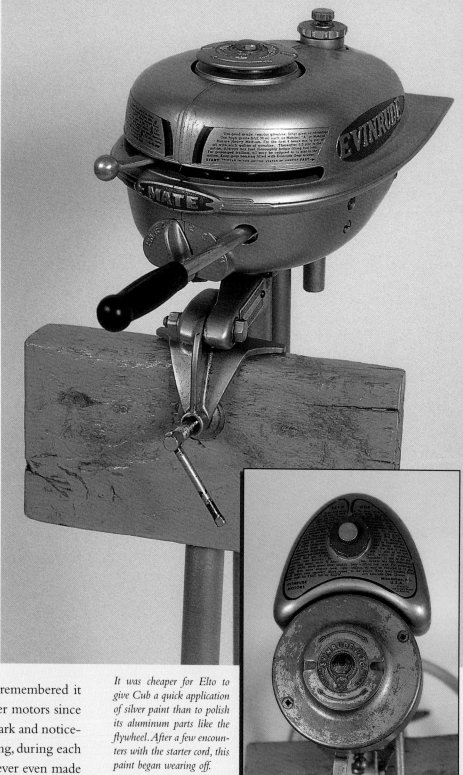

It was cheaper for Elto to give Cub a quick application of silver paint than to polish its aluminum parts like the flywheel. After a few encounters with the starter cord, this paint began wearing off.

Arguably, the Evinrude organization acted upon this conviction after their littlest engines' brief and final 1941 production schedule. Never again would they seriously think of offering a sub-one-horse outboard.

Ole's 'Ol Grandad of the Race Course

EVINRUDE "4-60"

Brand Name: Evinrude
Model: 4-60 Racer
Serial Number: (composite motor)
Year of Manufacture: about 1938
Manufacturer: Evinrude Motor Company
Place of Manufacture: Milwaukee, Wisconsin
Type: Two-cycle, Water-cooled
Number of Cylinders: 4
Bore X Stroke: 2-3/4" X 2-1/2"
HP @ RPM: approximately 60 @ 5000+
Weight: 138 lbs.
Original Price: $495
Owner: Robert Grubb

several racing motors in this book are not entirely the products of their listed manufacturers. That actually makes them more typical of the alcohol-fueled or "alky" racing genre than if they were simply "box stock." Our 4-60 fits nicely into the "concoction category" because racers have made modifications to at various times. In fact, this motor is likely the composite of several powerheads and assorted aftermarket parts. Every competition season, word would invariably spread that a winning engine had some new homebrew improvement. Sometimes by the very next race, similar hop-ups appeared on rival drivers' motors. There are even reports of victorious engines with a purple carburetor, for example, suddenly spawning similarly colored carbs

Here's the view of 4-60 that racers with "slower" motors saw. The fuel tank, in official Evinrude/Elto racing orange, has a fully opened air vent. Failure to give it a good twist could result in vibration closing it and curtailing fuel supply. Note lower right piston and rings peeking through the aftermarket open exhaust stacks! This motor sings quite a tune, especially when burning alcohol-based fuel mixed with castor oil.

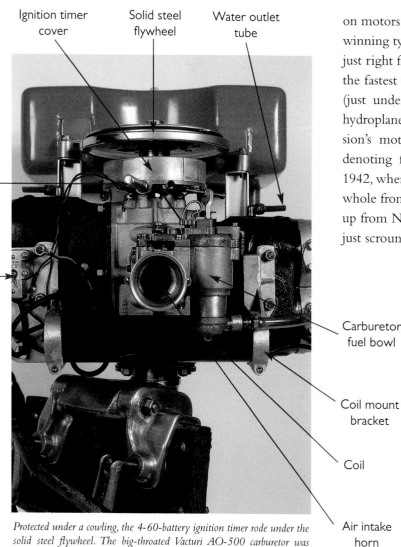

Ignition timer cover · Solid steel flywheel · Water outlet tube

Timing lever

Ignition switch

Carburetor fuel bowl

Coil mount bracket

Coil

Air intake horn

Protected under a cowling, the 4-60-battery ignition timer rode under the solid steel flywheel. The big-throated Vacturi AO-500 carburetor was standard issue on most 4-60 mills from the mid-1930s onward. Adjusting the needle valve while looking back during high-speed running could be quite a trick. A glance or two was mandatory, though, as the driver had to check for cooling water flow from the little telltale pipes on the cylinder tops.

on motors of jealous foes. All other things being equal, winning typically resulted from a "magic" prop shaped just right for that day's racecourse conditions. Some of the fastest of these wheels were prepared for Class "F" (just under 60 cubic inches displacement) outboard hydroplane racing. For nearly three decades, this division's motor of choice was the Evinrude 4-60 — denoting four cylinders and 60 cubic inches. After 1942, when these big engines were no longer available whole from Evinrude, racers were known to whip one up from Navy surplus, small outboard racing shops, or just scrounged parts.

The 4-60 traces its roots to those three experimental double Elto Light Twins that Ole Evinrude pieced together in 1923. More directly, though, one should begin the lineage with the 1928 Elto Quad. Its constant shower of competitive kudos convinced the Evinrude family that big motors could generate giant publicity through speed records. As soon as the original Evinrude Company had been reacquired, Ole's group stacked a pair of 30-cubic-inch Speeditwins to create a 60-cube monster capable of besting all comers. Released for 1930, this model #178 could be purchased with an Elto, Evinrude, or Lockwood decal — something that can confuse a new collector today. However, the tag common to all of these badge-engineered versions also indicated that the motor was an Outboard Motors Corporation product. Even today, historical references list the early 4-60 as an "OMC Racer." However, by the mid-1930s, the 4-60 was fully labeled as an Evinrude product. It was winning too many races to be associated with the firm's economy Elto division (and Lockwood was discontinued in 1932).

Cylinder heads on the early 4-60 were flat and not detachable from the cylinder casting. Hence, they're referred to as "flatheads." However, the brain trust in the Evinrude R&D shop paid close attention to ways that race drivers were getting extra spunk from their 4-60s. Mid-season factory nuance changes (of carbs, bearing placement, etc.) were common and netted more speed. For 1935 through 1941, the 4-60 was fitted with detachable cylinder heads like those on our subject motor. This allowed mechanics to shave a bit of metal off the heads for extra compression.

The 4-60's official fuel tank color had long been "racing orange" and, as the factory had hoped, this was unmistakable in any crowd of boats. Unfortunately, the alcohol and castor oil fuel mix typically burned by these mills made quick work of both paint and labeling. "Alky" motors were not officially available from the factory, as even the 4-60 in stock form was a conventional gasoline and oil motor. But, company officials readily expected buyers to immediately tear down their new purchases in order to widen fuel passages for alcohol use, and add the latest "secret" parts during the process.

Evinrude identified each 4-60 (and many of its other motors) with a small rectangular tag on the transom bracket and a matching set of numbers stamped in the crankcase. For various reasons, lots of racers pulled off the former tag and some obliterated the latter. Another confusion source is the fact that Evinrude sold lots of 4-60 powerheads to midget racecar owners. Some found their way back to the water and had to be connected to a "parts" lower unit (possibly still wearing its ID tag). Consequently, it's often difficult for an outboard collector to accurately pinpoint a specific racing motor's pedigree. In antique outboard circles, this has come to be accepted reality.

The owner of the photographed 4-60 supposes his motor to be a close relative of the 1938 model 8005. Numerical identification is missing, but its detachable

cylinder heads and lower unit are consistent with this estimate. A 4-60 built up with pieces from some wayward post-World War Two 50-horse Evinrude is also a possibility. The 1946 and 1949 Big Four powerhead was essentially a 4-60 anyway. Only when a racing motor was either retired early or only used in informal competition will it be found in relatively "factory stock" condition. The author has a 1930 vintage 4-60 #178 0409 that somehow managed to get into a small summer community in northern Ontario, Canada where, for decades, it was occasionally passed along from one young lakeside "cottage racer" to another. By the 1970s, an impecunious schoolteacher had picked up the old 4-60 to power his garden-variety fiberglass runabout. Throughout this whole time, the motor lived free of the frequent surgery inflicted upon motors drafted for serious competition.

Getting set for a race, the 4-60 driver would squirt some fuel directly into the big Vacturi carb's air horn. With the battery switch on, spark advance lever in proper right-of-center position, and rope wrapped securely around the flywheel, the cord is given a committed pull. As soon as the motor started, the driver quickly opened the throttle past its half-open starting position. Then, with the boat up on plane, carb adjustment would be smoothed out, and the water tubes exiting each cylinder bank checked for cooling water flow. Nice-running engines that had the bugs worked out prior to race day allowed the driver to concentrate on the buoys and crowded course. Hopefully the fuel tank was full. Running out of alcohol at over 60 mph meant the castor oil was gone, too! That's like having the brakes slammed on and often resulted in seized pistons.

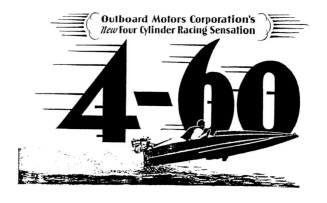

EVINRUDE BIG FOUR

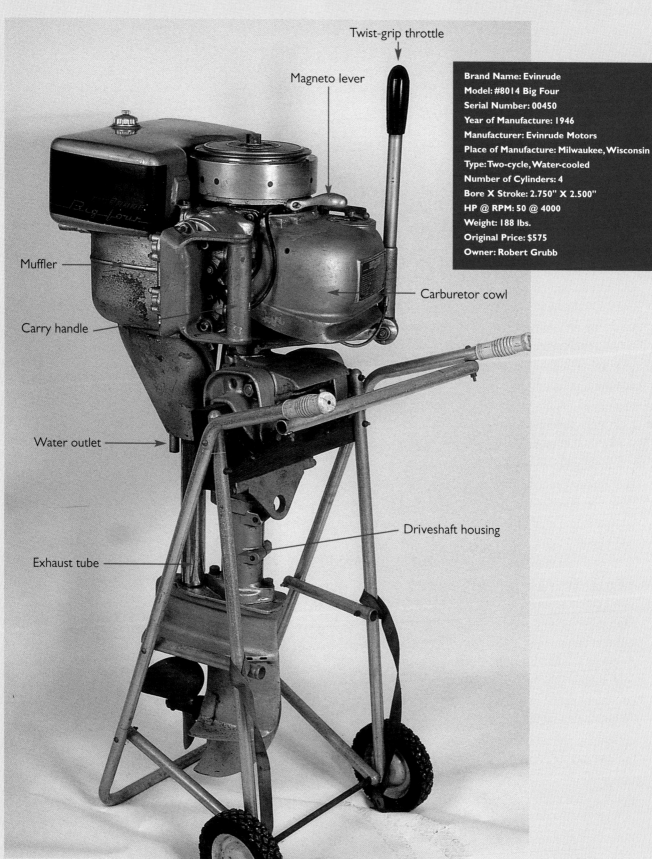

Twist-grip throttle

Magneto lever

Muffler

Carry handle

Water outlet

Exhaust tube

Carburetor cowl

Driveshaft housing

Brand Name: Evinrude
Model: #8014 Big Four
Serial Number: 00450
Year of Manufacture: 1946
Manufacturer: Evinrude Motors
Place of Manufacture: Milwaukee, Wisconsin
Type: Two-cycle, Water-cooled
Number of Cylinders: 4
Bore X Stroke: 2.750" X 2.500"
HP @ RPM: 50 @ 4000
Weight: 188 lbs.
Original Price: $575
Owner: Robert Grubb

Many of the motors in Evinrude's 1946 catalog were fast approaching obsolescence. Like a wide range of the period's consumer products, most were just there as a way of requesting people to *please stand by.* After all, the company had legitimate reasons for filling its early post-war sales literature with revamped pre-war outboards. Aggressive 1942-1945 government contracts had sidetracked Evinrude's civilian research and development. Dealers hadn't been able to obtain a new motor much past April 1942. At war's end, a scramble to get America back to peacetime production led to material shortages, aluminum included. And the victorious public — survivors of a long economic depression, as well as four years of a world war — was ready to spend pent-up savings on American goodies like cars, homes, boats, and outboard motors. No major manufacturer was offering a new outboard design for '46. A few of the smaller outfits, such as Flambeau, introduced unique engines, but brand loyalty still made good sense to average folk. They wanted the kind of motor they'd admired before the war and perhaps saw pushing small military craft in movie newsreels. Especially from 1945 to 1947, Evinrude (and Johnson, et al) dealers had lengthy customer waiting lists and frustrating engine allocation schedules. The then recently popularized GI expression "Snafu" (situation normal, all fouled up) was a patriotic way of blaming delays and shortfalls on government red tape. Accepted snafus that kept most of the same old larger Evinrudes in the catalogs through 1950 actually served to buy the organization time to develop the user-friendly outboards responsible for starting the great family boating and water-skiing boom.

Albeit based upon some passe technology, the 1946 Evinrude line possessed remarkable range from "1.1 to 50 certified horsepower," as their virtually unnecessary advertising indicated. The Big Four, our subject motor, reigned from the far right of that spectrum, but seemed a reclusive king. Only occasionally featured in company ad copy, the mammoth 188 pounder took a back seat to its much smaller "fishing-size" sisters that most of the market craved. Oft mentioned last, if brought up at all, the 'Big Four' was "for powering fastest outboard runabouts, cruisers, big utility boats," period literature briefly noted.

Wartime promotion had treated the huge motor's

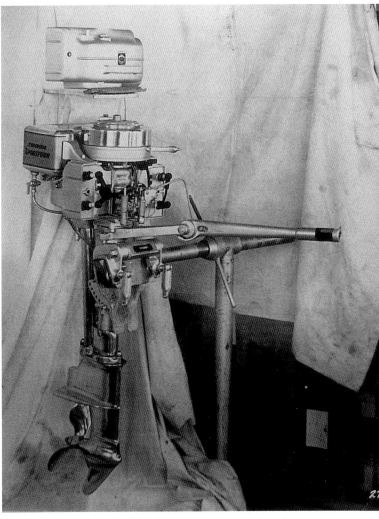

This factory photo of a 1934 Evinrude Sport Four Imperial shows front cowl removed from a motor just pulled from the assembly line. With 16.2 horses, this four had nearly 35 less horsepower than Big Four, but, during its run, sold many more units than its larger brother. Evinrude knew that, through the early 1950s, the larger the motor, the smaller its potential marketplace would be. Carefree aluminum and fiberglass family runabouts, full-shift outboards, and the popularity of water skiing changed all that.

immediate predecessor with greater respect. In June, 1943, for example, the firm's public relations people proudly touted "Evinrude Power for swift Storm Boats." This headlined an artist's rendering of what in retrospect is an obvious Big Four racing eight combat-ready US soldiers to a war-torn beach. "Storm Boats" they're called," the copy patriotically explained, "these slashing little hurricanes of power and speed. They can float in mere inches of water. They can weave, twist, dart like furious hornets. And they can whisk a landing force to a beach in a breath taking hurry . . . Victory is our sole job now . . . with peace there will be brilliant new Evinrudes for happy days on the water again."

In fact, the Storm Boat motors had been built with Evinrude 4-60 racer powerheads, a magneto — as opposed to battery — ignition, a cowl with beefy carrying handles, and a rugged lower unit. While it is not clear how many saw action, it can be said that some made it into the active, post-war surplus marketplace at home and abroad. The Evinrude organization having a history of fiscally conservative wisdom, likely considered excess Storm Boat motor inventory a minor windfall, as Uncle Sam had funded the project. In any event, the company saw fit to replace the military model's craft-specific transom mount with a regular-use thumbscrew bracket. It also shifted from olive drab paint to Evinrude silver with blue decals, and issued a civilian model number (#8014). The erstwhile Storm Boat motor — now dubbed "Big Four"— was listed in the 1946 catalog. Evinrude knew that people would be clamoring for motors, admittedly mostly rowboat sized. But, this revamp was probably done in the spirit of, "Well, we've got the Storm Boat Motor parts we might as well use them. And, we shall see what we shall see."

What happened was that a few thousand adventurous souls bought them. Among this corps was the overall winner of the prestigious Albany-to-New York Marathon and other daredevils looking to rig up the fastest outboard boat on their particular waterway. Tiny snapshots of some of the unique high-speed craft offered in 50 cent plan form by the delightfully diverse *Boat Builder's Handbook,* hinted that Big Four provided perfect power for these go-for-broke designs. The big motors also found a home on the transoms of more than a few home-brewed houseboats. Most Big Four activity, though, probably took place in dockside bull sessions during which young marine buffs concocted boat and motor "dream teams" with the powerful Evinrude jetting some small, sporty hull. A comparatively few Big Fours actually showed up in mundane shoreline life.

Fifty horsepower represented a lot to handle in the Big Four's no-gearshift format. The operator had to be quite certain of a clear path ahead before pulling the wraparound starter cord. I recall being teenaged ballast in the bow of a Big Four powered 14-foot aluminum rowboat. The driver, having stood in order to gain "yanking advantage," nearly fell overboard when the motor started, and I hung on for dear life. Eventually all of the full-race Vacturi brand's carburetor adjustments were smoothed out and fear subsided into manageable anxiety. Suffice it to say, though, such shotgun starts — the province of Big Four — are not for the fainthearted. Neither was the model's price tag. At nearly six hundred bucks in 1946 money, a consumer might choose between Big Four and a complete rowboat/3.3 horse fishing motor/trailer/rod and reel combo, or between this top-of-the-line Evinrude and a decent down payment on a house!

One can safely assume that sundry engines in 1946 Big Four production lasted in various showrooms beyond the official model year. The 50-horse Evinrude had enough of a champion at the executive level, however, to be reissued as the #8015 in 1949. By then, pricing had jumped to $645. That year, too, it never seemed capable of managing more than mere footnotes in colorful Evinrude advertising. Buyers were primarily stock outboard marathon racers aiming at some prizes or well-to-do single guys figuring to make a statement. It is believed that leftovers could be easily found into the early 1950s. No doubt they became very tough to sell at anywhere near list price. Evinrude's wonderfully-designed Big Twin 25 hit the market in 1951 and delighted large motor buyers with its compact, streamlined appearance, rewind starting, reliable performance, remote fuel tank, and, above all, the full gear shift. Though only half the Big Four's rated power, the new Evinrude (and Johnson) 25 horse outboards immediately made the company's large, opposed cylinder, rope-start models the province of a bygone era.

The Red Head's Orphan

RED TOP

Brand Name: Red Top
Model: none designated
Serial Number: 0008
Year of Manufacture: 1946
Manufacturer: Auto City Outboard Association, Incorporated
Place of Manufacture: Detroit, Michigan
Type: Two-cycle, Water-cooled
Number of Cylinders: 1
Bore X Stroke: 2.250" X 1.750"
HP @ RPM: 4 @ 4000
Weight: 45 lbs.
Original Price: unknown
Owner: Robert Skinner

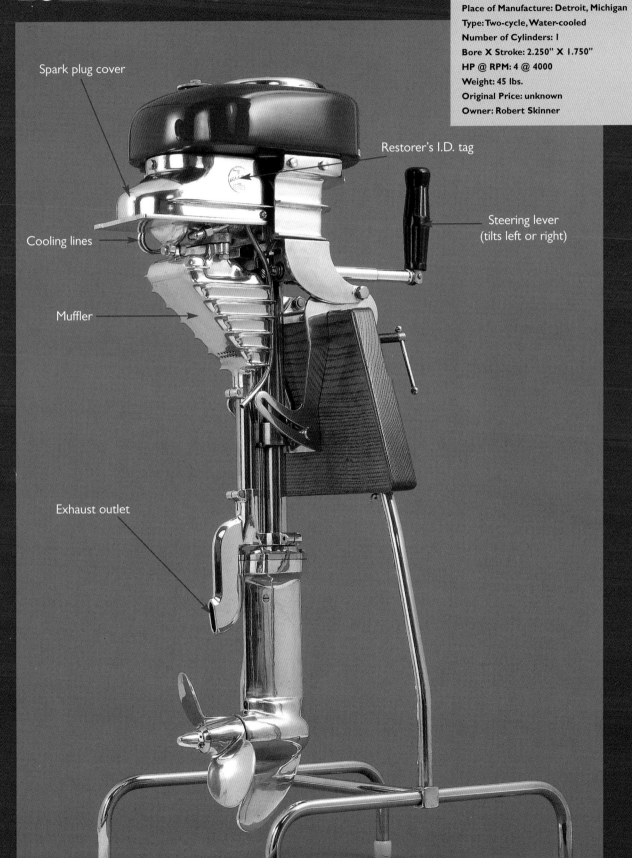

Spark plug cover

Restorer's I.D. tag

Steering lever
(tilts left or right)

Cooling lines

Muffler

Exhaust outlet

Before reading further, please put a marker here, and consult the pictures of the book's Caille Model 15. Then check the vintage Caille catalog page in this section, too. Apparent similarities are some of the only remaining clues as to the origin of our featured Red Top motor. Antique Outboard Club member Bob Lomerson began the detective work on this rare brand in the 1980s after being dogged by the faint memory of a tiny outboard maker near his Pontiac, Michigan boyhood home. Eventually, he and another enthusiast were able to meet an elderly man who had been part of the little enterprise around 1945. Reportedly, a couple dozen moonlighting Packard car workers established the Auto City Outboard Association with a plan to build fishing motors sure to be popular in the imminent peacetime marketplace. Estimates of the number actually produced range from about 27 to 250. Legally, the manufacture of civilian recreational products, such as outboard motors, was prohibited by the War Production Board between spring of 1942 and late 1945. Consequently none could be openly advertised for sale until 1946 without Uncle Sam having a conniption fit. It's doubtful Auto City had much of a promotional budget anyhow.

Besides its attractive casting work, colorful crimson tank, and compact rewind starter, the Red Top's very unique vertical steering grip garners attention. To turn the motor's lower unit, one pushes the grip down to the right or left, as if engaged in arm wrestling. Meanwhile, the powerhead continues facing forward. Lomerson speculated that the Red Top represented a clever revamp of one of Caille's last models. The author concurs with this suggestion, believing the Auto City group stumbled upon the remaining Caille inventory about a decade after that red fuel tank-bedecked line was discontinued.

Considering the motors' physical similarities, Auto City's and Caille's common Detroit venue, as well as the fact that stock from defunct makers didn't get deep-sixed as quickly as is the case today, it is logical to

It's doubtful that assemblers in the tiny Red Top factory sent their outboards out the door with this beautiful brand of shine! Red Top was meant to be a low budget, but reliable kicker. Note "A/C" logo that the AC sparkplug people might have called into question had the motor been widely distributed.

assume Red Top has a Caille lineage. The Red Top looks to be a fine product. Our subject motor is said to perform as well or better than comparable major brand outboards of the period. Why the small business closed before properly introducing its wares will no doubt be forever open to question. Should the entire Red Top stock have been built predominately from fire-saled obsolete Caille parts, however, it may be conjectured that Auto City was neither in a financial nor legal position to have additional components cast for further production.

Compare the Red Top with the Caille in this 1930s catalog. Now, see if you agree that there's some connection between the two brands.

For Those Who Prefer Catching Fish Four-Cylinder Style

EVINRUDE ZEPHYR

Brand Name: Evinrude
Model: Zephyr #4404
Serial Number: 26198
Year of Manufacture: 1948
Manufacturer: Evinrude Motors
Place of Manufacture: Milwaukee, Wisconsin
Type: Two-cycle, Water-cooled
Number of Cylinders: 4
Bore X Stroke: 1-1/2" X 1-3/8"
HP @ RPM: 5.4 @ 4000
Weight: 43 lbs.
Original Price: $182.50
Owner: Arthur DeKalb

*Lots of "conveniences" were packed into a Zephyr including a gas cap that
one didn't have to bother venting with a little knurled vent screw. Instead,
air was piped in from under the hood. The rewind or "Simplex" starter also
sold many of these "Cadillac of fishing motors."*

"Make sure nobody sees ya," the marina owner told his young summer help. "Just dump 'em about a couple miles out and get back here for another load." That Southeastern Connecticut Evinrude dealer was referring to small, four-cylinder outboards he wished had never crossed his shop floor. Even though these 5.4 horse mills hadn't been in the catalog for several years, they still seemed to be popping up all over the place, their aggravated owners storming into his dealership demanding better service. By the mid-50s, he simply made a practice of offering more trade in allowance than these little quads were worth, and then had his gopher deposit them in Davey Jones' Locker. Once there, they'd never again waste his mechanic's time on fussy ignition or carb work that would only prove temporary and thus free of charge.

Of course late 1930s Evinrude engineers had no intention of causing such consternation when aiming for the world's smoothest running fishing motor. Their efforts yielded an engine that ran away with much of Evinrude's 1940 through 1949 ad budget and later filled Antique Outboard Motor Club flea markets to overflowing. Its name was to be so specially representative of the fishing and cruising fun promised by the motor, that a contest was established to find the perfect identity. An imaginative Evinrude employee won a motor for envisaging a soft, carefree, gentle wind or "zephyr" kissing a happy young couple as they Evinruded o'er a cool, cedar-shorelined, blue lake.

The new Zephyr was part of Evinrude's fine-tuning as the premier brand in the new (in 1936) Outboard Marine and Manufacturing Corporation triumvirate; Evinrude, Johnson, and Elto. It allowed the marque to boast four, four-cylinder motors in an eight model line. At 5.4 horses, Zephyr was the most popular of this foursome. It was rightly sized for the average 12 to 14-foot rowboat or runabout and accepted by many outboard consumers as an amazing little quad of high quality and reasonable price. Each was equipped with a convenient rewind starter, too. Zephyr ads almost always included at least one smiling angler holding up

Magneto lever

Carb adjuster

Needle valves

Anti-backfire device

Fuel bowl

Stuffed under a Zephyr's front hood were four sparkplugs, a carb with anti-backfire unit, linkages, and enough adjustment screws and knobs to satisfy even the most ardent tinkerer. In 1949, Evinrude offered the model with weedless angled prop or "fisherman drive" lower unit design.

a lengthy string of huge fish. Or, a pretty woman in a colorful swimsuit was shown enjoying Zephyr's reliability. Even some of the advertising admitted this kind of imagery looked or sounded "almost too good to be true! But take the word of delighted Zephyr owners from coast to coast that *it is true!*" Evinrude promotion consistently plugged the "wonderful smoothness of 8,000 balanced, overlapping power strokes [in the four little cylinders]. per minute." Zephyr literature also promised "exceptional starting ease! Thrilling responsiveness, and flick-of-the-throttle flexibility from slow trolling glide to surging top speed!"

How well did a real Zephyr run? The ads were relatively correct. It was indeed a remarkable little outboard. A well-maintained Zephyr started quickly, went right along (but no faster than a twin-cylinder five-horse rival), could idle mighty smoothly, and be an overall joy to own. Like any other model, some were just "golden." In time, though, if you hadn't happened to have bought a "lucky" Zephyr, or cared little about clean fuel, ignition points, carburetor needle valve adjustments, sparkplug changes, and other routine maintenance, it could make for one miserable machine.

A retired Evinrude official once mentioned to me that so many engineers were falling over each other while trying to outdo one another during the Zephyr project (and subsequent upgrades) that such sensitive components as the carburetor and ignition system were over-engineered. Still, the motor sold well and the Zephyr may be considered as Evinrude's cornerstone during the entire 1940s decade. Even in wartime, a military version was produced for life raft propulsion.

In 1950, three-quarters of Evinrude's fours disappeared from the catalog, and then vanished altogether the following year. By 1952 every Evinrude was an alternate-firing twin advertised as the way to go in modern outboarding. This sharply contrasted with the old message about Zephyr's four, opposed, smooth-running cylinders being best. Each successive boating season, the little quad looked more and more out of place. Second, third, or fourth generation owners, grew less patient with Zephyr's complex carb and aging four-wire ignition system. Problems with these older engines were especially pronounced in places like southeastern Connecticut where salt water loved devouring little metal parts.

By 1960, fewer and fewer dealers welcomed ailing, geriatric motors. Perhaps due to its ubiquity, the Zephyr became the poster motor scapegoat of this broken down legion. Had it been a vintage four-cylinder motorcycle engine, or small stationary engine, Evinrude's micro-four (with only 9.7 cubic inches of piston displacement) might have found quick haven in antique power buffs' collections. But, the Zephyr's original success made it a victim of being too plentiful and too common. So far, old outboard hobbyists have tended to eschew the model. In a 1982 *Antique Outboarder* article, one buff expressed nearly universal sentiment by stating, "In regard to Zephyrs as a whole: I could never see the need for four cylinders to get 5.4 hp. These motors are so numerous and so undesirable from a collector's point of view. I decided to put them out of their misery, especially if they were frozen. I would reduce them to salvage or scrap. And so I write the requiem for the Zephyrs. I hope they don't become an endangered species because of me."

The writer also hopes the Zephyr doesn't become endangered. After all, the diminutive quad truly represents a milestone in Evinrude history and is reminiscent of a vibrant American industrial credo promising that more stuff is better than less stuff. So, Zephyr #4404-26198, once received by the author as a bat-

tered hulk, was given to a fellow old motor buff who enjoys revitalizing lost-cause engines. In fact, he turned it into the motor shown here!

Most Zephyrs had rewinds, but this prewar edition was pure rope start. A catalog suggestion to "toss your cares in a foaming wake," was later taken literally when one dealer deposited troublesome old Zephyrs in Long Island Sound.

A Genuine Bargain!

ELGIN AIR-COOLED SINGLE

Brand Name: Elgin
Model: 571.58301
Serial Number: 301.2742
Year of Manufacture: 1946
Manufacturer: West Bend Aluminum Company
Place of Manufacture: Hartford, Wisconsin
Type: Two-cycle, Air-cooled
Number of Cylinders: 1
Bore X Stroke: 1-1/2" X 1-3/8"
HP @ RPM: 1.25 @ 4000
Weight: 20 lbs.
Original Price: $56.50
Note: Sold through Sears, Roebuck and Company stores
Owner: Robert Grubb

Besides having a fresher outboard design than Evinrude or Johnson in 1946, Sears' motors could be had for just a few dollars down payment. Credit was fast losing the stigma it wielded in pre-World War Two America. Besides, when dealing with a huge, out-of-town head-quartered retailer like Sears, consumers weren't actually asking to borrow money from folks they knew. Suddenly, paying by the month was becoming as patriotic to the accelerating economy as taking a home mortgage. That shifting paradigm certainly moved a lot of Elgin outboard motors! The fact that the little green kickers were typically pretty darn good runners didn't hurt either.

Sears and Roebuck initially got into the outboard game in 1914 with a rebadged Lockwood-Ash rowboat motor. The arrangement lasted until sometime in the early '20s, and was followed by Muncie-built outboards that Sears rebadged as its Waterwitch line. By 1936, however, Sears decided it wanted a unique outboard line. A new Waterwitch was designed and Sears arranged to have the motors built by what remained of the Kissel car company. Many of the new Waterwitches were fitted with a patented twin pod or Mae West fuel tank that caused the motors to be visually quite distinct.

Post-war, Sears was anxious to update the styling and reliability of their outboards for the much-anticipated outdoor recreation boom. It was to develop a more modern motor that Sears signed a sizeable deal with Kissel's successor, West Bend Aluminum, for a completely reengineered line. In 1946, Sears offered four fishing motors in 1.25, 2.5, 3.5, and 5.5 horsepower denominations. The most expensive cost only $125 yet it and its stable mates were arguably the finest private-brand outboards offered up to that time.

Our subject Elgin was the least powerful of the debut line. It differed from its bigger sisters in that this 1-1/4-horse model was air-cooled. Even the era's littlest Elgin, though, exhibited remarkably sleek industrial design. A svelte lower unit and geometrically pleasing fuel tank contributed to what could arguably be termed the year's best looking outboard brand. Admittedly, this Elgin's air-cooling system wasn't completely without detractors. A few owners complained of engine overheating at sustained slow speeds although West Bend had aggressively finned both the cylinder and exhaust output section. Also occasionally problematic were the engine's tiny reed valves. Having no reed stops, they tended to break. But that was only likely if a propeller pin sheared and the powerhead was carelessly allowed to rev awhile without a load. No matter, Sears didn't have much patience with products that generated mixed reviews. The little Elgins were not allowed back in the catalog for 1947.

While there is some evidence of heat discoloration just below our pictured Elgin's exhaust fins, the cylinder and cylinder head paint looks to have kept much of its original finish. When tested for the *Antique Outboarder* in 1982, it demonstrated amazingly economical fuel consumption (one ounce per 10 minutes) and smooth, cool speeds from under one to a bit over four miles-per-hour. The motor's past ownership records are non-existent, giving license for historical fiction. We can speculate that either it has very low hours or overheating was never a problem with number 301.2742. It wouldn't be far fetched to imagine a responsible sixth-grader as this Elgin's first owner. With 20 or 25 dollars saved up from doing plentiful odd jobs during the last year of the war, a youngster could have easily put some money down. Maybe there was a Grandpa there to help with the order form and a pocket that magically produced several five-dollar bills. A paper route would have covered the balance in monthly installments. That still left lots of time for exploring coves of the local lake with his old flat bottom rowboat, coffee can bailer, and trusty little Elgin. Of course, there's got to be a water-loving pup in the mix, too. That would be just the kind of imagery Sears would utilize to get people to "Buy now! Pay later."

A company that made waterproof spark plug caps depicted their cartoon mascot on top of an Elgin. The motor was both generic and highly recognizable.

ELGIN AIR-COOLED SINGLE   83

Classic Sea Horse Green

JOHNSON TD

Brand Name: Johnson
Model: TD-20
Serial Number: 535837
Year of Manufacture: 1946
Manufacturer: Johnson Motors
Place of Manufacture: Waukegan, Illinois
Type: Two-cycle, Water-cooled
Number of Cylinders: 2
Bore X Stroke: 1-15/16" X 1-1/2"
HP @ RPM: 5 @ 4000
Weight: 40.5 lbs.
Original Price: $140
Owner: Arthur DeKalb

Webster's could have used the TD-20 to define "trusty fishin' motor." Very simple, user-friendly controls on this five-horse include combination needle valve/push down primer (on side of rewind assembly), easy access fuel shut-off valve, synchronized spark/gas "speed" lever, and sturdy rewind starter with metal pull handle. The nut protruding from the rewind assembly held spring innards in place better than one simply anchored into a thread in the actual rewind top. A rear handle (just under the lower cowling) and little wings on the tank ring front make for nicely balanced toting and resting the motor once you get there.

Johnson and Evinrude's parent company encouraged sibling rivalry. Through about 1950, each line was obviously distinct from the other. Except for certain fiscal opportunities — ones in which big money could be saved by sharing the cost of raw materials and sundry items like bolts — the two regarded each other as competitors. Evinrude, as elder sister, got to be the trendsetter. Johnson was encouraged to maintain its "dependability" reputation. Loyalists at both factories aimed for corporate parental approval sure to be lavished upon the first division to make one million outboard motors. The TD from Johnson made the firm a real contender.

Introduced in 1941 as the TD-15, this virtually immediate classic traced its ancestry to the 1930 alternate firing twin A-50, and through upgraded four-to-five-horse Johnsons in the 1937-1940 LT (Light Twin) and DT (Deluxe Twin) series. Each was a fisherman favorite, serving to define a trusty relationship between outdoors person and outboard motor. For many small boat owners of the 1940s and 1950s, though, Johnson's TD became the icon of the dependable fishing engine genre coveted by every competitor. In fact, the company adeptly used the motor's image to best represent its highly successful "dependability" market positioner. Johnson debuted the engine as if it had been faithfully standing by for years. In 1941, ads asked: "Why has Johnson's 5.0 horsepower model increased so fast in sales, [setting] one new sales record after another for the past four years?" Such business history referred to LT and DT, as well as the first few months of active TD orders. Johnson answered the ad's question stating that the TD "is the ideal all-purpose motor." The rest of the copy also serves us well, giving contemporary readers insight as to why one would choose to spend his or her money on a TD.

"Johnson's exclusive combination of perfected alternate firing and dual carburetion [via an extra breather valve] provides a full range of smooth power flow. The motor weighs only 42 pounds and this includes Ready-Pull starter — as well as full streamlined protection — from top to bottom. [Other features include]: underwater exhaust, *Synchro-Control* [single lever spark/fuel] *Rubber Rotor Force* [cooling water] pump, Rubber Flow shock absorber drive, Co-Pilot steering, oversize gas tank, and it is the only outboard of its size and type that has reverse!"

While the trademarked components had rather superfluous, proprietary names, their actual functions were indeed worthwhile. For example, during the TD's early catalog years, its buyers no doubt appreciated the "Co-Pilot" steering. They were likely accustomed to a motor with little discipline to stay on course whenever a hand momentarily left the tiller. Johnson made a nice correction on this simple peccadillo. Handy, too, was the reversing feature. Albeit completely the province of swinging the outboard 180 degrees, it did make the boat go backwards or, with engine silent, made for one of the easiest fuel refilling jobs on an integral tank motor. Of course, TD jockeys had to be quick on the steering grip for a graceful reverse. Otherwise the boat could tip to the side. And, once the half-rotation was complete, speed control, operated by reaching over the hood to the magneto/carb lever, was backwards! Ambidextrous challenges aside, Johnson received high praise from all kinds of people for their dependable performer.

Our photographed TD-20 hails from 1946. Unlike many of its competition in early postwar years, the TD did not appear outdated. Sea green paint (replacing a silver finish) gave the engine's attractive lines an even more comfortably modern look. And, in some unspoken way, the TD still had that classic Johnson provenance that naturally drew customers to the product.

The TD not only showed up on multitudes of transoms, but it made the pages of countless boat catalogs proud to present such an association. Even the simple brochure of a tiny, pond-side northern New York campground included a postage stamp-size line-drawn TD, rowboat, and angler captioned "Vacation Paradise." The motor was also used in a late 1990s brokerage house commercial with an "enjoy the good things in life" theme.

Designed and built well, Johnson's TD remained a standard bearer in the lineup through 1949 when a sister motor, the neutral clutch-equipped TN, took over for the engine's final four year catalog run. In late 1952, even Evinrude officials were impressed when Johnson rolled its one-millionth outboard off the busy assembly line. While a bigger Sea Horse 10 received the related press coverage, no one would deny that models TD and TN contributed mightily to a production figure never before achieved by any rival.

The Alky Racer's Fountain of Youth
HUBBELL

Brand Name: Hubbell
Model: C-52
Serial Number: 112
Year of Manufacture: 1952-1954
Manufacturer: Randolph Hubbell, et al
Place of Manufacture: South El Monte, California
Type: Two-cycle, Water-cooled
Number of Cylinders: 2
Bore X Stroke: 2.750" X 2.520"
HP @ RPM: 43-45 @ 6000
Weight: approximately 113 lbs.
Original Price: $625
Owner: Robert Grubb

S ignificant backorders for standard use motors like the Model TD convinced Johnson not to reintroduce racing motors in 1946. For high-performance outboard buffs, that meant an end to new supplies of the very fast Johnson PR, a Class "C" (30-cubic inch) leader since 1930. Try as they might, racers couldn't move Johnson or Evinrude off its decision to concentrate solely on family service engines. Enter Randolph Hubbell. Enthusiastically granted licensing to manufacture pre-war style Johnson and Evinrude racing parts, the California outboard speed buff and machine shop owner began supplying the professional racing community with components needed to keep their old mills spry and convert military surplus pump engines and outboards (like Storm Boat motors) into race-ready machines. Pros differed from the late 1940s "stock" outboard racers in that their mills were revamped to burn alcohol and castor oil fuel (as opposed to a stocker's pump gas/oil).

By 1950, Hubbell was able to offer a Johnson PR clone called the C-50 (1950 era Class "C" size) that he could make with his own and readily-available Johnson parts (like gas tanks, magnetos, and transom clamps). Hubbell metal-stamped serial numbers in the lower rear portion of the crankcase. When available, these were original Johnson components, but sometimes Hubbell cast clones. Origin of the motor's elaborate gear-driven external rotary valve parts had similar explanations. "C" sized Hubbells were also introduced in 1952, 1955 and 1960 as C-52, C-55 and C-60 respectively. They differed from the C-50 in nuances

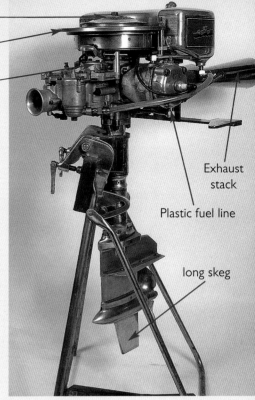

Fly wheel

Scatter ring

External gear-driven rotary valve assembly

Exhaust stack

Plastic fuel line

long skeg

Made with a mix of Hubbell, Johnson, and other parts, this Hubbell C-52 exhibits its gear-driven, half-speed external rotary valve between the big Vacturi carburetor and the crankcase. The "scatter ring" around the flywheel is designed to provide the driver with at least some protection should the high-revving aluminum flywheel mounted on a steel hub let go. The C-52's stacks represent an early attempt at tuned exhausts. Most "alky" (alcohol-based fuel) racers fed the carb with a see-through plastic fuel line like the one pictured herein.

of upgraded components and design changes. The longer skeg on our photographed engine is an example. The change took into consideration state-of-the-art drag-reducing, surfacing propeller technology where the motor is high enough out of the water to allow only one prop blade at a time to be submerged.

The featured C-52 exhibits the mix-n-match proclivities of many professional outboard racers. It wears cylinder heads from H.H. Fuller, another aftermarket performance supplier, and a "scatter ring" to protect the driver from disintegrating fragments in the event ultra-high RPM started breaking up the flywheel. Megaphone stacks were probably also add-ons, as tuned exhaust technology became popular after the C-52's initial release.

Hubbell's enterprise remained busy into the 1970s, turning out a variety of racing outboards. Some of these mated scrounged up Evinrude Big Four powerheads to high-speed lower units, yielding a Hubbell 4-60 offering. Others sprang from E. Carl Kiekhaefer's Mercury racing engines. Though willing to craft specialty motors from either the Evinrude/Johnson or Merc designs, Randolph Hubbell most enjoyed helping the former best the latter. Around 1960, Johnson's parent corporation, Outboard Marine, decided to reenter the high-performance scene long enough to wrestle a world's speed record from Mercury. OMC called Hubbell for one of his little shop's sleek lower units.

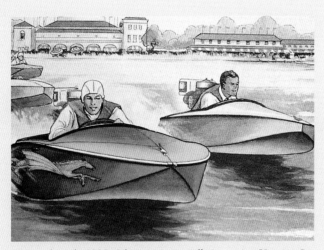

During the early 1930s, Johnson was especially into racing. Here is a Sea Horse outboard competition motif from the company's main catalog.

Putting Stock in Outboard Racing

MERCURY KE7 LIGHTNING, MARTIN "60" HI-SPEED, AND MERCURY HURRICANE KG7Q

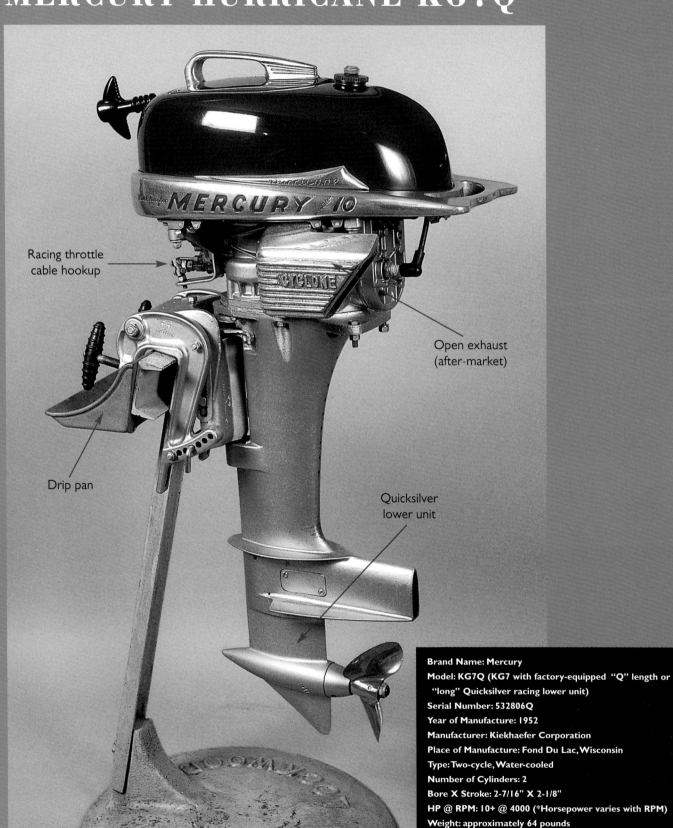

Racing throttle cable hookup

Open exhaust (after-market)

Drip pan

Quicksilver lower unit

Brand Name: Mercury
Model: KG7Q (KG7 with factory-equipped "Q" length or "long" Quicksilver racing lower unit)
Serial Number: 532806Q
Year of Manufacture: 1952
Manufacturer: Kiekhaefer Corporation
Place of Manufacture: Fond Du Lac, Wisconsin
Type: Two-cycle, Water-cooled
Number of Cylinders: 2
Bore X Stroke: 2-7/16" X 2-1/8"
HP @ RPM: 10+ @ 4000 (*Horsepower varies with RPM)
Weight: approximately 64 pounds
Original Price: approximately $275
Owner: Robert Grubb

Stock outboard racing burst onto the North American boating scene in 1946. The sport was ready-made for baby-booming families possessing even the most modest craft, a 10-horse outboard, and a desire for some friendly competition without much fuss afterwards. In fact, the genre was championed by folks who loved the idea of being able to use their boat for fishing on Saturday then race it Sunday afternoon. Stock racing clubs, both formal and ad-hoc, sprang up most anyplace home to even a puddle of a waterway.

The Neenah, Wisconsin Boat Club was one of these fledgling organizations that endeavored to stage a stock outboard marathon in 1947. That October's *Lakeland Yachting* reported everything was going fine with the happy group of traditional Evinrude and Johnson owners. "Classes for [their] races [were] established according to motor horsepower ratings" of the garden variety 9.7 horse Evinrudes, 9.8 hp Johnsons, and other rather evenly-matched denominations of those mainstays. "But," the magazine revealed in news scoop style, "the introduction and popularity of the Mercury 10 hp Lightning has played havoc with these ratings." It seems that motors like the one in our picture were messing up lots of fair-weather competitors.

When E. Carl Kiekhaefer decided to scrap the crude outboard designs found in the old Thor plant, he set out to engineer a motor with a fuel tank that would look like a streamlined fastback car, have a sleek lower unit, and a powerhead delivering more zip than even the most critical outboarder might expect. Associate Merlyn Culver wanted Kiekhaefer to replace the Thor name, too. Culver convincingly suggested the fleet-winged mythological Mercury's identity to label the line, and several well-performing models made the new brand a quick, critical success for 1940 through early 1942. War work allowed Kiekhaefer to develop his earlier vision using some of Uncle Sam's money. The government had awarded Kiekhaefer a defense contract to produce a 20-cubic inch, twin-cylinder, 12-horse chainsaw motor. His passion for reducing engine friction caused the fledgling Wisconsin industrialist to include ball or roller bearings everywhere possible.

The resulting well-received, air-cooled chainsaw powerplant got revamped into water-cooled form at war's end. It was introduced as the Mercury's Model KE7 for the 1947 boating season. Although the out-

The first fast Mercs, KE7 Lightnings, quickly spawned even faster successors like KF7 Super 10, and Super 10 Hurricane model KG7. Shown on this 1952 catalog page is the standard Hurricane on a regular "fishing" lower unit. Few buffs, however, bought these hot little mills primarily for trolling.

board — soon dubbed Lightning — tested as high as 12-15 horsepower, Kiekhaefer demanded the new motor only be called a 10. He would deftly use such underrating tactics to amaze buyers and embarrass the heck out of the companies he believed were out to get him, namely Evinrude and Johnson. Adding fuel to this fire was the issue of incompatible horsepower rating standards. Johnson and Evinrude went by Outboard Boating Club (which Kiekhaefer suspected was controlled by his chief rivals) guidelines allowing for "peak" or best burst power grading. Mercury used stricter Society of Automotive Engineers requirements awarding specific horsepower marks only for longer term, "continuous duty" performance.

What racing clubsters like those in Neenah, Wisconsin soon discovered was that a loosely rated Johnson 9.8, for example, was no match for the new Merc 10 which was really at least a true 12 that could rev a lot higher than the older design Johnsons and Evinrudes any day. When one of his new Lightnings beat everything in its class at the famed 1947 Albany-to-New York Marathon, Kiekhaefer jumped aboard the stock outboard bandwagon with ardent fervor. Within a few weeks of that Hudson River race, KE7 became stock's Class "B" (20-cubic inches of piston displacement) standard. Mercury's publicity department parlayed victory after victory into ads stressing "speed and stamina." Of course, outboarding's main market was still the family fishing crowd, so promotion also included Lightning's ability to troll as well as propel a light hull at 30 miles per hour.

crankcase, and heftier porting than KE7. Typically, nobody with any other kind of 10 to 16 horse motor could catch up with a boat being pushed by one.

Then George Martin decided to hop-up a little poppet valve fuel induction outboard that his Eau Claire, Wisconsin firm had marketed to docile anglers.

Actually, Martin didn't own the company that produced motors bearing his name. He licensed his clever mechanically controlled poppet valve technology to the National Pressure Cooker Company (later called National Presto Industries) and headed its outboard division. Introduced in 1946, Martin's cornerstone engine was dubbed the "60" as, in blueprints, it looked to yield about 6.0 hp. In dynamometer testing, though, the compact powerplant consistently hit 7.2 at an easy 4000 RPM. Those poppet valves insured efficient fuel introduction at all speed settings, thus enabling remarkably lazy trolling and quick getaways without the hesitation of some other designs. Word in the sportsman community spread that Martin made a darn good fishin' motor.

With that, sales took off, and George Martin had breathing room for a little experimentation in the R&D shop. He'd been an outboard racing buff for several decades, so had a good idea how to tweak the "60." His guinea pig engine was soon hitting 16 hp when fueled with an alcohol/caster oil mix! By fall 1949, Martin had mated one of his wild "60" powerheads to a short, super-streamlined "torpedo" lower unit and entered it into a Minnesota stock outboard championship event. Mr. Kiekhaefer was there to see his Mercs clean up. What he witnessed was the little 11-cubic inch Martin "60" (then running on regular pump gas/oil) "blowing the doors off" of boats equipped with 20-cube Mercury Lightnings! Angrier than a bothered hornet, Merc's CEO stormed over to Martin and demanded an explanation. The grinning

Brand Name: Mercury
Model: KE7
Serial Number: 194714
Year of Manufacture: 1947
Manufacturer: Kiekhaefer Corporation
Place of Manufacture: Cedarburg, Wisconsin
Type: Two-cycle, Water-cooled
Number of Cylinders: 2
Bore X Stroke: 2-7/16" X 2-1/8"
HP @ RPM: 10 @ 4000
Weight: 59 lbs.
Original Price: $275
Owner: Robert Grubb

A beautiful package inside and out, the KE7 became synonymous with this brand of versatile performance. When the Michigan Wheel Company began marketing high performance, two-blade props (trademarked: Aqua-Jet) for the likes of the Lightning, it meant even more speed was possible with what was essentially a family-use outboard. Thousands sold, their crates often eagerly being pried open by an excited teen, as Dad and the local Mercury dealer watched with a smile. the KE7 was updated for 1949 as the Lightning Super 10. This one had a different carb, bigger opening from carb-to-

victor silently tipped up his "60" revealing the full-race lower unit. Kiekhaefer had subscribed to early stock rules authorizing only regular or "fishing" lower units. But, Martin's actions made the Mercury man determined to follow suit. Back at the plant, E. Carl Kiekhaefer hollered for his engineers to devise a racing lower unit gearcase that could fit on existing Merc driveshaft housings. And, he wanted it quick!

The legendary Quicksilver racing lower unit resulted. Offered originally as an accessory gear case, the "Quickie" was soon available only with a specially matched "tower" or driveshaft housing that easily bolted to KE7 or KF7. A larger version came on the market for the four-cylinder in line, 40-cubic inch Merc introduced in 1949. By the end of summer 1950, Quicksilver equipped motors dominated their classes. This essentially sank the original regular service "utility" boat/motor spirit of stock outboard racing, as "Quickies" could not be used on the family runabout for fishing *and* racing. Nor were they operated without a special "deadman's" throttle and steering wheel. And a "Quickie" motor was a couple of inches shorter — from transom clamp to prop shaft — than regular lower unit motors. This was unsuitable for craft with standard, 15-inch transoms. Bottom line, without a super sleek Quicksilver lower unit, one could not hope to win in Merc-dominated classes. Family service boat and motor-style stock outboarding was effectively finished off in 1951 when E. C. Kiekhaefer's company made a complete racing motor package by marketing its recently released 20-cubic inch KG7 on a "Q" length "Quickie." This was labeled KG7Q on the fuel tank ring-mounted ID plate and

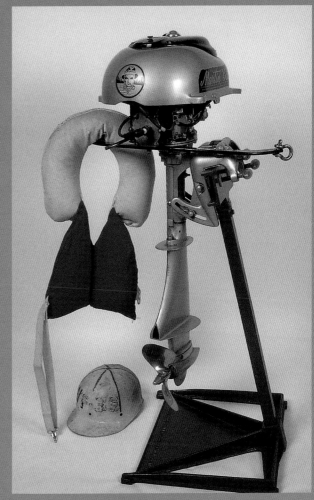

When set up to run on an alcohol/castor oil cocktail, these diminutive motors required one to don helmet and life jacket. A good "60" Hi-Speed "alky" motor would hit 16-hp, lots of zing for an 11-cubic inch motor. Note the "Marty Martin" fisherman logo on the fuel tank. Any fish that could hit bait at this outboard's speeds would probably also enjoy swallowing the boat!

engine block. This model (and its standard lower unit mounted sister, KG7) was dubbed the "Super 10 Hurricane." It had meatier intake/exhaust porting, and eight reed valves where its ancestors wore four. A decent "Hurricane" could dyno test on speaking terms with 18 hp. Consequently its underrated specs sported an asterisk indicating that the 10 horses would likely jump with high RPM.

More than any other modern maker, Mercury loved to devote at least a few catalog pages to tooting their "innovative" horn. Even a glance at their early 1950s outboarding technologies verifies that the company had a right to brag.

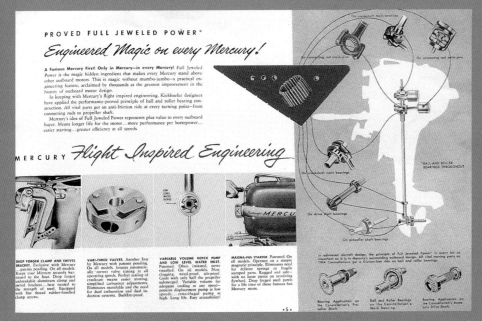

PROVED FULL JEWELED POWER®

Engineered Magic on every Mercury!

A Famous Mercury First! Only in Mercury—in every Mercury! Full Jeweled Power is the magic hidden ingredient that makes every Mercury stand above other outboard motors. This is magic without mumbo-jumbo—a practical engineering feature, acclaimed by thousands as the greatest improvement in the history of outboard motor design.

In keeping with Mercury's flight inspired engineering, Kiekhaefer designers have applied the performance-proved principle of ball and roller bearing construction. All vital parts get an anti-friction ride at every turning point—from connecting rods to propeller shaft.

Mercury's idea of Full Jeweled Power represents plus value to every outboard buyer. Means longer life for the motor...more performance per horsepower... easier starting...greater efficiency at all speeds.

MERCURY *Flight Inspired Engineering*

DROP FORGED CLAMP AND SWIVEL BRACKET. Exclusive with Mercury ...patents pending. Keeps your Mercury securely fastened to the boat. Drop forged unbreakable aluminum clamp and swivel brackets...heat treated to the strength of steel. Equipped with fine thread rubber-handled clamp screws.

VARI-TIMED VALVES. Another first by Mercury with patents pending. On all models. Insures automatically correct valve timing at all operating speeds. Perfect sealing of crankcase means easier starting, simplified carburetor adjustments. Eliminates manifolds and the need for dual carburetion and dual induction systems. Backfire-proof.

VARIABLE VOLUME ROTEX PUMP AND LOW LEVEL WATER INLET. Patented. Often imitated, never equalled. On all models. Non-clogging, weed-proof, silt-proof. Cools with only half the propeller submerged! Variable volume for adequate cooling at any speed-positive displacement pump at low speeds...centrifugal pump at high. Long life. Easy accessibility!

MAGNA-PUL STARTER. Patented. On all models. Operates on a simple magnetic principle. Eliminates need for delicate springs or fragile stamped parts. Rugged and safe—with no loose pieces on revolving flywheel. Drop forged steel pawls for a life time of those famous fast Mercury starts.

In advanced aircraft design, the principle of Full Jeweled Power is every bit as important as it is in Mercury's outstanding outboard design. All vital moving parts on TWA Constellations get a friction-free ride on ball and roller bearings.

"BALL AND ROLLER BEARINGS THROUGHOUT"

Bearing Application on the Constellation's Propeller Shaft.

Ball and Roller Bearings on the Constellation's Main Bearing.

Bearing Application on the Constellation's Accessory Drive Shaft.

Brand Name: Martin
Model: "60" Hi-Speed
Serial Number: CHS 1135
Year of Manufacture: 1950
Manufacturer: Martin Motors Division of
National Pressure Cooker Company
Place of Manufacture: Eau Claire, Wisconsin
Type: Two-cycle, Water-cooled
Number of Cylinders: 2
Bore X Stroke: 2" X 1-3/4"
HP @ RPM: 7.2 @ 4000
Weight: - 43 1/2 lbs.
Original Price: $275
Owner: Robert Grubb

KG7Q pilot had the boat up on plane, the so-called underwater exhaust snout screamed unobstructed, anyhow, just about the waterline. The featured engine (p.88) looks to be ready for an "outlaw" stock event, in which standard American Power Boat Association rules were bent to suit enthusiasts at non-APBA sanctioned races. Running open exhausts sure sounded like fun. In fact, the "Cyclone" add-on not only made for greater noise, but probably contributed an extra mile or two per hour to the deal.

By 1952, the "Q" length lower unit gave way to the "H" or Hydro-short "Quickie" even a bit shorter than "Q" and sized right for the small transoms on stock out-boarding's recently added hydroplane (as opposed to runabout with passenger front seat) class. The "H" Quicksilver unit can be distinguished from the "Q" version by absence of "Q's" top cavitation plate just above the exhaust section. The KG7Q was replaced by the KG7H. Along with this model and the standard KG7, a KH7 entered the catalog in 1952. This "Super 10 Hurricane" was fitted with Mercury's first forward-neutral-reverse gearshift and given the added title "Cruiser." Within two years, an even more powerful 20-cubic inch Merc racer, the Mark 20H, threw its older high-performance sisters into quick obsolescence. Happily, though, many of these motors, while passe to serious racing devotees, were sold off to a new group of informal, young "cottage racers." These folks and their homebuilt boats were ready-made for the power still pulsing in an old Merc Lightning, wayward Martin "60" Hi-Speed, or Mercury KG7Q.

KG7Q motors, like their regular service KE7, KF7, and KG7 sisters were sold with cowling covering the whole powerhead. Most lower shrouding, however, was removed by owners who either wanted their mills to resemble racers' stripped-down motors or desired instant access to sparkplugs, carb and other components. Of course, that's why race drivers discarded them, too. Lack of shrouding also allowed an early owner of our pictured KG7Q to install an aftermarket "Cyclone" open exhaust stack. Most stock rules forbade such direct from cylinder-block output, mandating underwater exhaust only. Interestingly, though, when a

JOHNSON MODEL RD

Brand Name: Johnson
Model: RDE 16 - Sea Horse 25 Electric
Serial Number: 1135673
Year of Manufacture: 1954
Manufacturer: Johnson Motors
Place of Manufacture: Waukegan, Illinois
Type: Two-cycle, Water-cooled
Number of Cylinders: 2
Bore X Stroke: 2-7/8" X 2-3/4"
HP @ RPM: 25 @ 4000
Weight: 111 pounds
Original Price: $498
Owner: Arthur DeKalb

By 1950 Johnson and Evinrude were in the midst of what appeared to be a perpetually increasing commitment to deliver product. Their parent organization, Outboard Marine and Manufacturing, had its hands full with these stars as well as with busy outboard plants in Galesburg, Illinois (where the economy line Gale Buccaneer was being cranked out by the thousands) and at the firm's burgeoning Canadian operation in Peterborough, Ontario. Corporate talk got serious about breaking down the old Johnson vs. Evinrude cultures and having both offer what would essentially be the same line of motors, distinguished only via cosmetics. Loyalists at each factory sure didn't think this a very acceptable plan, but changing times called for business to be on a constant lookout for new ways to stay fiscally and promotionally healthy. One of the first joint efforts leading to this organizational streamlining, was the "25 project."

Reportedly, this Johnson/Evinrude 25-hp marriage was supposed to be eased into through a courtship only involving the co-development of a lower unit. Atop it would be a four-cylinder 25-horse model in Evinrude showrooms or a 25-hp twin-cylinder motor for Johnson 25 buyers. Such protocol could nudge the amalgamation on its way, while retaining the "deluxe" Evinrude vs. "sensibly dependable" Johnson tension that provided those product lines with palpable definition. Each was to share two highly successful features that Johnson unveiled in late 1948 on its model QD-10 Sea Horse 10; the remote fuel tank and forward-neutral-reverse gearshift. Having the gas tank separate from the engine allowed big outboards to be shrouded within a smaller package. It also made refueling and motor transport/storage easier and cleaner.

The shift empowered even the most inexperienced outboarder to better maneuver his or her craft, as well as eliminating the dubious requirement of starting the brute at better than half-speed forward. When finally set in motion, the 25 project's immediate pre-production phase included just the Johnson twin design. It was decided that the four-cylinder powerhead didn't perform as well as desired, and that it would cost more to build. So, within earshot of expected partisan cries, a joint 35.7 cubic-inch twin was authorized by Outboard Marine brass. A team effort was fostered whereby Evinrude workers would get to fabricate much of the new 25's guts (connecting rods, crankshafts, etc.), while Johnson people were responsible for die casting aluminum into various "25" components. Staff at the subsidiary Gale-Buccaneer plant also pitched in with items like carbs and the remote gas tanks.

The resulting motor was publicly announced during the fall of 1950 as the Evinrude *Big Twin* (a name both Evinrude and Johnson had previously used), and Johnson Sea Horse 25. Rival Mercury was already offering a 25 that was really a 40 horsepower motor, but it had no shift. Outboard shoppers went nuts about the Evinrude and Johnson new gearshift 25, instinctively understanding how it would change their family boating experience for the better. They swamped dealers with orders by year's end. *The Boating Industry* April 1951 edition revealed that the 25s were finally being

A little scratched, but you would be too if every summer since 1954 you pulled kids on water skis, had weedy fishing line wrapped around you, got socked by lures, paddles, and skis, and then smashed your foot on rocks near the shore. Note the Sea Horse 25's gear linkage for the tiller arm twist grip speed control. Big knobs on the faceplate were a popular design in the early 1950s as they were reminiscent of the large dials on expensive radios and TV sets.

Because even the Johnson and Evinrude advertising people didn't yet envision the huge family outboard cruising and water ski market, the first Sea Horse 25 catalog renderings focused on anglers.

brochure pictured an old angler, hands outstretched in a "that big!" pose conferring dependable fishing motor status on Johnson's capstone engine. By the time our featured outboard came off the assembly line in 1954, however, fishing had taken a back seat to other family boating pursuits like water-skiing. That year, Johnson was building motors around the clock with lots of the demand stemming from young couples — each with upwards of three or four kids — wanting to get towed on skis atop cool, shimmering waters.

One can intelligently argue that motors like our featured Sea Horse 25 really made water skiing practical. Prior to the full gearshift's introduction, children were not encouraged to learn to ski. With no real idling or neutral capabilities, earlier "big" outboards could yield some pretty scary helmsmanship and close calls to waiting skiers bobbing not far from boat and propeller. The new 25s — with shift and great idling — allowed water-skiing to be casually sampled by millions of folks. That turned the sport into a national pastime as the starting signal *"Hit it!"* was heard on lakes and rivers throughout the country. The Sea Horse 25's two large cylinders served to provide sufficient torque for water-ski take-offs. By the summer of 1951, advertising began depicting this activity in hyperbolic fashion with 25s pulling multiple skiers. One brightly colored shot was circulated showing seven people behind a 25 horse Evinrude-powered craft. Of course, the skiers were all petite bathing beauties on wide skis, but this sent a message to family motor shoppers that the 25 possessed tremendous potential for their gang.

shipped to distributors and dealers. Both brands were having a tough time keeping up with market demand. The magazine noted that "reports of [Sea Horse 25 and Big Twin] performance [were] being sent to the [Outboard Marine] firm from all over the country. Comments range from astonishment from the high speeds provided by the motor to the amazement of its trolling ability."

The Sea Horse 25, and its mechanically identical but somewhat differently shrouded Evinrude sister, were first marketed to the fishing market segment, as that had long been the outboard industry's biggest segment. Johnson's battle cry for the 1951 debut of the Sea Horse 25 was: "25 horsepower...Speeds over 30 mph, yet it trolls!" Even the 1952 Johnson

"Look Ma, no hands and no observer in the Big Twin 25-powered rowboat!" The full-gearshift Evinrude and Johnson 25s made water skiing a family sport. Their two big cylinders pounding away gave adequate torque for pulling even "bigger" folk and multiple skiers out of the water.

CHOICE OF THE CHAMPIONS!

Bruce Parker, America's top-flight water skiing champion, is an enthusiastic Big Twin owner. "Words can't describe Big Twin's fine performance, but the record speaks for itself," says Mr. Parker. Here is the record! In 1952, Big Twin powered Bruce to 8 notable titles. His skiing partner, Evie Wolford, to 8 titles. And both, in doubles events, to 2 titles. Here is Bruce and his trophy-laden troupe at the '52 National meet, American Water Skiing Association, Minocqua, Wisconsin. (From left) Barbara Goode, Eastern Girl's Champion; Bruce Parker, National Senior Champion; Evie Wolford, National Slalom Champion; Jim Myer, Eastern Boy's Champion.

Besides capitalizing on the remote six-gallon fuel tank — of which well-prepared outboarders might have two or three — and gearshift, these 25s were the first modern outboards to incorporate electric starting and quickly attached remote shift/throttle levers. Along with a steering wheel, these features allowed for the motor to be started and controlled from anywhere in the boat. Most importantly, the conveniences brought large numbers of women into the role of outboard boat skipper, a handy assignment when Dad wanted to take a turn on the water-skis. The Sea Horse 25 (and Big Twin 25) electric starter was offered by both Johnson and Evinrude as a built-in option for 1954. Twin lever Johnson Ship Master (and Evinrude Simplex) throttle/shift remote controls had already made a splash in previous catalogs. Each was only considered novel for a very short time.

Our subject Sea Horse represents a good original-condition motor discovered on a dealer's back rack. Visible is its three-pin fuel connector that mated to a female connector from a twin-hose (air pressure and fuel) *Mile Master* fuel tank. With its thick black plastic cap secured, this container was airtight. Prior to starting a cold motor, the operator would depress a small thumb button on the tank assembly in order to deliver some fuel to the carburetor. Once running, the engine's crankcase pressure was sent down the air hose to pressurize the tank. Erstwhile young shipmates might recall their folk's 25 conking out about 1000 yards from shore because someone forgot to tighten the cap. There will also be those who can close their eyes and hear the long-ago "whoosh" sound of air being allowed to escape the tank as that cap was loosened at the end of the boating day. Failure to carry out this little chore could result in a burst hose.

Below the fuel connector, a tiny throttle control hook reflects the sunlight. Our Sea Horse 25's jagged voltage decal is intact, indicating it's Johnson's top-of-the- '54-line electric starter model. Long gone with its last wooden boat, are the steering deck-mounted "start" and "choke" buttons (there was no ignition key), as well as the small, three-sided solenoid cover box that attached to the inside transom. It, too, wore a Johnson electric start logo. Nicely positioned handles front and aft added to the model's portability, although most of these outboards were purchased to stay mounted on a small outboard cabin cruiser (where

two often found homes) or the likes of a 15-foot-and-change lapstrake Lyman runabout. The handle in back of the main Johnson decal could facilitate opening a hinged rear door that provided access to the sparkplugs. But, a screwdriver was necessary for this short procedure.

In 1955, Outboard Marine (which officially became Outboard Marine Corporation or OMC) was still selling its respective 25s at an enviable clip. Competitor E. Carl Kiehaefer, however, had been enticing some big outboard shoppers with his 40-horse, four-cylinder engines. Now also featuring a shift, Kiekhaefer's larger Mercurys pestered OMC into an exciting horsepower race. For the following year, The Sea Horse 25 (and related Evinrude) was updated with another five horses, then an extra five on top of that in 1957. Soon a 25 seemed small. Even so, the revolutionary motors had done a big job in helping create the 1950s (and beyond) boating boom. Truth is, more than a few of these outboards, including the one shown here, are still in service today.

An Oddball Trying to Crack a Conventional Market

FLAMBEAU

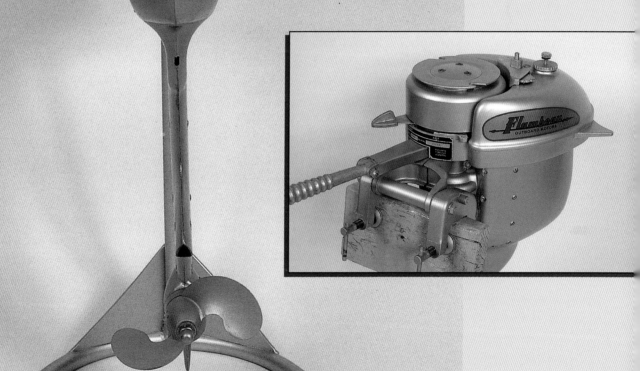

Brand Name: Flambeau
Model: 5-46-1
Serial Number: 2638
Year of Manufacture: 1947 or 1948
Manufacturer: Metal Products Corporation
Place of Manufacture: Milwaukee, Wisconsin
Type: Two-cycle, Water-cooled
Number of Cylinders: 2
Bore X Stroke: 1-15/16" X 1-9/16"
HP @ RPM: 5 @ 4000
Weight: 34 lbs.
Original Price: $163
Owner: Robert Grubb

Inset: Flambeau advertised its engines as being "truly outboard" and indicated this would keep the boat free from dripping fuel. The EPA would love that! The little screw receptor casting beside the "fast" marking is there to fasten the optional rewind starter. While this one wears a "finished" rope sheave plate, many other standard rope start Flambeaus simply have one designed for the rewind "catchers," and look like something is missing.

Sandwiched between stunning OMC and encouraging Mercury postwar sales successes were a raft of also-ran outboard makers that paddled along before throwing in the towel by 1960. While many offered truly attractive, innovative products, most got sampled only because new (1946 to early 1950s) Evinrudes, Johnsons, or Mercs were in high demand, but relatively short supply. Smaller, rural, and/or newly established dealers were most especially in the belly of this marketing dilemma whale. They stood little chance of getting significant quantities of the majors' motors. Consequently, when the sales rep from some miniscule maker came knocking, these retailers were apt to sign up. Among the modest brochures, promotional signs, and display motor or two to enter these shops, were those of the highly unconventional Flambeau.

Milwaukee's Metal Products Corporation was headed by veteran outboard racer George Kuehn. It was somewhat of a family affair with his brother and a couple of other seasoned outboard men as principles. Among the group, Leo Kincannon had experience in outboard motor design, and was responsible for putting Flambeaus on the drawing board. Actually, Metal Product's original plans were to have Kincannon go to Cedarburg, Wisconsin to help with the design transitions from Thor to Mercury to Flambeau.

In 1940, the Metal Products people had made a purchase offer for the fledgling Kiekhaefer Corporation. While it initially appeared the transaction would go through, Carl Kiekhaefer (then just a minor stockholder trying to market his newly-conceived Mercury line at the New York Boat Show) got wind of this "hostile takeover" attempt, and raced back home to nix the deal. Had he not acted so quickly, Merc might have become Flambeau (or visa-versa) and boating history would be very different indeed.

It's likely that Flambeaus were designed during the war, as two-thirds of the line was ready in 1946. The firm's debut roster included a 2 1/2-hp single, a twin with double the single's rating, and a large twin said to generate 10 hp. The big flambeau hid out in boating magazine specs through about 1947 and was never heard from again. Actually, only one or two of these were built as prototypes for display or testing. The author has a Golden Flambeau Ten that shows some signs of factory experimentation, little running time, much dragging around, and lots of nicked gold paint. Other than a set of decals, it doesn't appear to have had any identification of model or serial number, typically hinting of a machine that never got into the marketplace.

To say the least, none of the line bore any resemblance to Mercury, or any other contemporary. On drafting paper and in person, the resulting Flambeaus were alluring outboards . . . sleek as well as compact. Kincannon designed the motor to take advantage of the kind of simple sandwiching that Thor Hansen had used with his steel stamping Thors. Rather than use Thor's easily corroded cadmium steel, though, Kincannon had left and right sides of the Flambeaus — from the cylinder tray(s) on down to the lower unit skeg — cast in high-quality aluminum.

The assembly process involved placing parts into one of the half's recesses, mating the other half on top, and then bolting the halves together. Also cast in pairs, top and bottom and of aluminum was the fuel tank. Flambeau's proprietary carburetor got connected to the tank's underside, thus being invisible to the operator. One did have carb access, however, via primer, fuel shut-off, and needle valve adjustments terminating on top of the tank near its gas cap. High and low speed carburetor settings were geared together and would be fine-tuned in unison. Vintage outboard buff J. L. Smith decided to crack open a Flambeau to critique it for a 1988 *Antique Outboarder* article. That strange carburetor amazed him the most.

"This patented dual carb is in effect two carb systems contained within one body. The systems are located on either side of the carb and apart from drawing fuel from the centrally located float basin, act independently, each having its own adjustment, jet air intake, and delivery passage to the cylinder(s). The high speed could be compared to the automotive type using main downdraft induction with high-speed mixture adjustment, butterfly valve and nozzle. This section of the carb also has an idling jet called 'intermediate jet' in [Flambeau] brochures which acts the same as the idling mixture of a regular carb. The low speed system or secondary carb receives an independent supply of fuel from the float basin, has its own adjustment and jet, air intake and path to the cylinder(s). The passage is smaller than that for the high speed and arrives at the intake bypass on the opposite side by a separate opening." Most models had no choke.

Without meaning to be facetious, it may be said that most potential buyers choked on the thought of owning a Flambeau. Especially during the 1950s family boating boom, a strong word-of-mouth network of brothers-in-law, know-it-all neighbors, and the Jones' next door could negatively impact sales of second-string brands. When that make happened to be filled with features as unconventional as its name, companies like Flambeau really faced uphill battles. Metal Product's outboards suffered from a modest dealer network. Eventually many delare aquired Evinrude, Johnson, or Mercury franchises. The clever Flambeau design, originally its biggest selling point, eventually became its largest liability. With fewer and fewer shops willing to offer repair of the strange bird, ailing Flambeaus tended to be relegated to the far back rack where reluctant mechanics made excuses about parts not being available. More than one frustrated owner tried affecting his own repairs only to have pieces mysteriously tumble from somewhere in the left or right half upon experimental disassembly. Few marinas had anyone willing to spend time on such triage, and the motors were left to their fate in some oil-soaked cardboard box typically exiled to a storage shed.

Most Flambeaus found today or already in collections, hail from the 1946-1950 period. For the latter year and through to their end, Flambeaus were treated to a reddish burgundy powerhead area and silver lower unit. A plastic finish was heated into the coloration, causing some to now display a yellowed patina. Horsepower was bumped to three and six respectively in 1950, but returned to the slightly smaller ratings the following year. For 1953, a cavitation plate was added to the thin lower unit. No matter, sales apparently dropped steadily from the very early 1950s through 1956 when Metal Product's executives decided not to further postpone the inevitable. Enough stock existed, though, for a few Flambeaus to be assembled and sold locally when the firm liquidated its outboard holdings in the late 1950s. Some four decades later, in a small, Milwaukee-area cement block building, a stash of factory parts and original motor blueprints was saved from the dump by an enthusiast who appreciated their value to marine propulsion history.

LIGHTNESS
AN UNEQUALLED
Flambeau
FEATURE

SINGLE — 2.5 H.P.
TWIN — 5 H.P.
OBC Certified
at 4000 RPM

★ *Lightness*
★ *Truly Outboard*
★ *No Shear Pin*
★ *Handling Ease*
★ *Compactness*
★ *Performance*

Every time you handle the Flambeau — you'll renew your appreciation of its light weight and compactness. Far lighter, the Flambeau 5 h.p. weighs only 32 pounds. Some outboards weigh as much as 50% more. Check these features and you'll agree with the thousands of enthusiastic Flambeau owners that a Flambeau Outboard Motor has the features you've always wanted. Write today for the amazing story of the new Flambeau.

OBC
Sustaining Member

METAL PRODUCTS CORPORATION
Dept. OL-495, 245 E. Keefe Ave.
Milwaukee 12, Wisconsin
Please send me FREE your new full color booklet on the new Flambeau Outboard Motors.

Name_____

Address_____

City_____ State_____

MARTIN "200"

Brand Name: Martin
Model: EHO
Serial Number: 9277
Year of Manufacture: 1953
Manufacturer: Martin Motor Division of National
Presto Industries, Inc.
Place of Manufacture: Eau Claire, Wisconsin
Type: Two-cycle, Water-cooled
Number of Cylinders: 2
Bore X Stroke: 2-1/2" X 2-1/32"
HP @ RPM: 20 @ 5000
Weight: 70 lbs.
Original Price: $359.75
Owner: Robert Grubb

ands raised in frustration on his way out, George Martin had exited his namesake outboard company before its most legendary motor was released for 1953. At 20 hp, the 19.94 cubic inch piston displacement Martin "200" represented double the power previously offered by the firm that enjoyed a solid fishing engine reputation. It was also one of the first times that a production outboard delivered a fraction over one horsepower per-cubic-inch. The limited edition OMC Speedi-Bee had done so in 1930, but under the auspices of an out-and-out racing job. Actually, an earlier Martin "200" yielding only 17 hp was slated for a 1951 introduction. Though a few prototypes were built and the model advertised, officials realized this one simply wasn't ready. Blame was placed on aluminum shortages spawned by the Korean War.

That said, George Martin had looked in on the group designing the early 20-cubic-inch powerhead and wasn't particularly happy with what he'd seen. Scuffling with National Presto Industries' brass while trying to keep things humming along in the outboard division, though, left him with little time for micro-managing. After Mr. Martin's departure, engine designer Gilbert "Tex" Sitz worked up the motor that debuted as the 1953 model "200." It was supposed to be offered in full gearshift, as well as forward-only versions. Ten shift-equipped prototypes, minus serial numbers, came off the line. It is unknown what happened to them, or why the forward-neutral-reverse "200" never hit showrooms. Publicity shots with a shifter "200" on an outboard cabin cruiser were taken at Chetek Lake, Wisconsin. Differences between the two versions of "200" were primarily in the lower unit and steering/speed/shift control tiller handle.

By 1953, any maker wanting to remain in outboarding's major leagues needed shift motors in the line. Martin had sold lots of fishing kickers from 1946 through the early 1950s, but thereafter found it increasingly difficult to stay at its upper Triple A league level once Evinrude, Johnson, Scott-Atwater, and Mercury began featuring gearshift outboards in their catalogs. Not that Merc was an old hand at the shift game. Kiekhaefer-produced F-N-R models for 1953 included only the Mark 15, a 10-horse, and 16-hp Mark 20, which turned out to be the leading Martin "200" rival. Martin might have done better to concen-

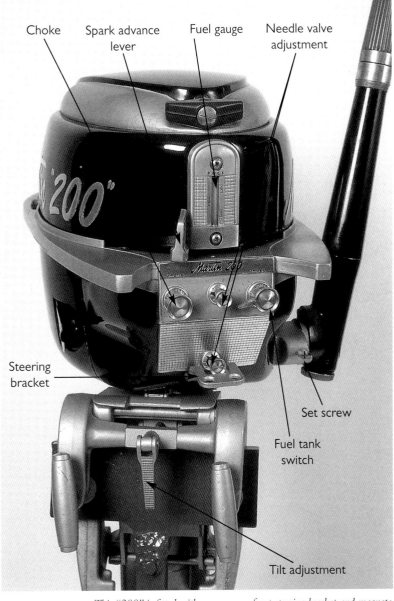

This "200" is fitted with an accessory front steering bracket and magneto /spark advance lever. The latter facilitated separate spark and throttle control, normally operated via the tiller's red plastic twist grip. The knob on the instrument panel's right switches fuel tank options. When the setscrew near the base of tiller is loosened, the plug-in tiller handle can be removed and a remote control piece inserted. Note the little fuel connector door on the left side of lower cowl. It allowed use of a remote tank.

trate on a shifting motor, but things were not completely copasetic in National Presto's outboard division. Talk started to circulate that motors were not necessarily sacred to the parent company's management. And it can be argued that, under the circumstances, the "200" released in 1953 symbolized the Martin outboard folks' best hope for survival. Better to issue a reliable forward-only model to the public than have a less-tested shift-equipped motor that might generate complaints. But the cancellation truly came down to the wire. Reportedly, a shift "200" made it to the 1953 New York Boat Show. And, *Popular Science* editors mentioned it via a rather complimentary write-up and picture in their January 1953 issue.

Our featured "200" is among the guesstimated 1,500 to 3,000 big Martins actually sent into circulation during 1953 and 1954. Catalogs distributed by late winter 1953, when the outboard buying season shifted into higher gear, identified the top-of-the-line model as "200" Silver Streak. This tied in nicely with the brand's black and silver motif. Interestingly, the brochures admitted that it was "built by speed experts, for speed lovers [and equipped] with its special Torpedo Lower Unit [that] skims the waves like a breeze [giving] you thrill after thrill as you show your wake."

Much of Martin's other ad copy clung to the "enthusiastic sportsmen" (meaning anglers, duck hunters, et al) theme. The "speed experts" terminology reveals a clue that Martin engineers, many of whom were stock outboard racing buffs, had bet the farm on Silver Streak's high performance opportunity to bring new glory to the jeopardized marque. And, it was initially done in such fine print that stockholders probably wouldn't have a chance to get suspicious about a surreptitious image change.

The "200" Silver Streak was bigger than necessary because of an integral fuel tank that it actually didn't need. A switch on the "200" instrument panel could dial in the motor-mounted tank or a six-gallon remote reservoir and related exhaust pressure-operated diaphragm fuel pump. This gave extra cruising range. The standard tank allowed for a slightly reduced "standard motor price," offered traditionalists comfort, had a built-in gauge, and did define the motor with styling that announced the "200" as a big boy. Conversely, Mercury's 20-cubic inch Mark 20 motor, slenderized by way of a remote tank and powerhead-hugging cowls, could be mistaken for a seven-and-a-half.

The 20-cube Mercs, and to some degree similarly sized motors from Minneapolis-based Champion Outboards, provided the Silver Streak "200" with its only real speed competition. "Tex" Sitz had deftly incorporated George Martin's mechanically controlled intake poppet valves into a remarkably smooth powerhead delivering a supple range from trolling to planing speeds. And that is what gave the "200" a Corvette-like performance image. Out of the box, the motor was a cottage racer's delight. Those who propped it to run up to 6500 RPM on a light hull hit bursts of 25 horsepower. Its sleek "Torpedo" lower unit gearfoot was on a par with Merc's full-race Quicksilver piece, and far more streamlined than the standard Mercury feet of KE-7 Lightning, KG-7 Hurricane, or Mark 20. Martin catalog's fine print made it clear that 15:16 gear ratio Torpedo came "standard on [all] Martin "200" Silver Streak motors." While a full-racing version — with shorter exhaust housing, and pointy gear case cap — appeared in a few places for 1954, the "200" Silver Streak's best work was done on the stern of bantam weight rowboats and small runabouts. With such partnerships, the big Martin was free to frustrate owners of more expensive craft and power. Alas, the model died in its prime when National Presto execs suddenly silenced the outboard division before 1954 could play out.

Martin Motors always played second fiddle to its parent company's main theme, Presto Pressure Cookers.

CHRIS-CRAFT RACER

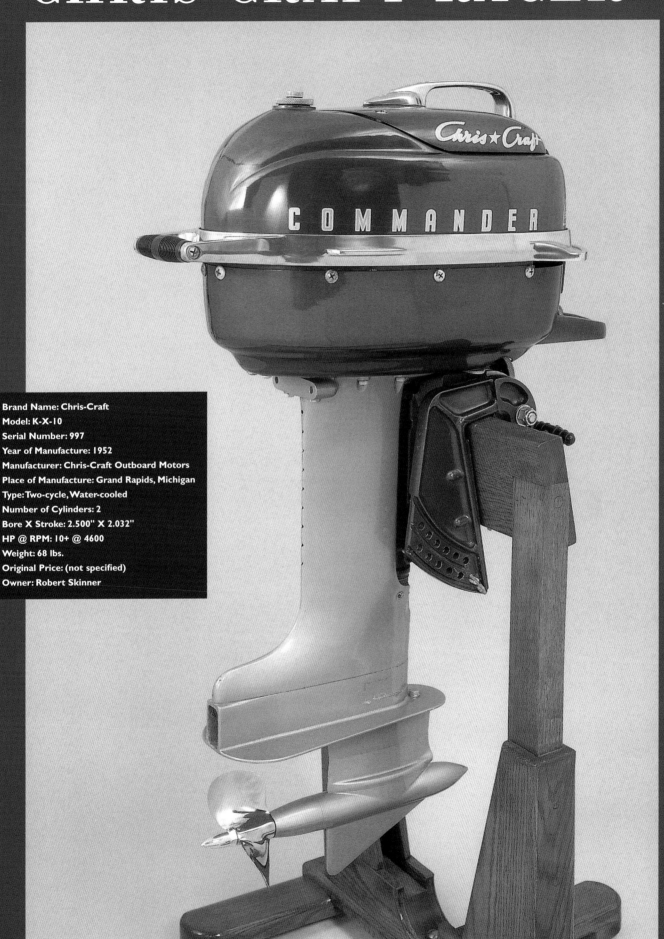

Brand Name: Chris-Craft
Model: K-X-10
Serial Number: 997
Year of Manufacture: 1952
Manufacturer: Chris-Craft Outboard Motors
Place of Manufacture: Grand Rapids, Michigan
Type: Two-cycle, Water-cooled
Number of Cylinders: 2
Bore X Stroke: 2.500" X 2.032"
HP @ RPM: 10+ @ 4600
Weight: 68 lbs.
Original Price: (not specified)
Owner: Robert Skinner

In 1951, about a dozen outboard manufacturers assembled an illustrated report on the necessity of motor use in American commerce. Among this brotherhood lobbying for a surer stream of materiel allocations in the midst of the Korean War were Chris-Craft and Mercury. This was an uneasy alliance. Little more than a year later, the two would be embroiled in a legal dispute that eventually knocked one of the early 1950s fastest-growing outboard lines out of the market.

It would have been easy for Chris-Craft brass to extend their prestigious boating image into the outboard motor market by simply private branding someone else's engines. There's no reason to assume that OMC or even Mercury, for that matter, wouldn't have jumped at the chance to badge-engineer product for Chris-Craft. After all, Outboard Marine was doing so by the tens of thousands (through revamps of its Buccaneer brand) for Montgomery Ward as well as for the oil company that is now Exxon-Mobil. And, Mercury generated steady income via its sale of Wizard motors to Western Auto Stores.

Any chance to be allied with the world's largest maker of high-quality pleasure boats would provide public relations opportunity indeed. But, Jay Smith

Certainly one of the nicest looking 20-cubic outboards ever produced, the 1950-1953 Chris-Craft Commander was the short-lived outboard division's fastest model. It would serve as the basis for half of Chris-Craft's proposed 40-cubic inch, 25-horse engine.

(son of Chris-Craft founder Chris Smith) wanted his outboard to be an original. Reportedly, plans for such an engine were discussed in the late 1930s, but with the war interruption, product wasn't unveiled for another decade.

What debuted was a 5 1/2-horse model dubbed Challenger. This nicely engineered, attractively stylized, and well-built 1949 offering gained quicker acceptance than any other contemporary newcomer in its class. A 10-hp Chris-Craft, from which our subject motor is derived, was introduced in 1950. This Commander model, too, was a rather easy sell in the 20-cubic inch arena. Both motors could be matched with a hull from Chris-Craft's new group of reasonably priced plywood kit boats. A Commander and its parent company's 10-foot racing pram represented a speedy relationship ubiquitously pictured in period boating magazines and arguably the envy of many youthful cottage racers. When the likes of this combo began winning some stock outboard events, Chris-Craft officials decided to spice-up their 10 with several powerhead modifications and a streamlined lower unit to keep current with rival Mercury's new Quicksilver gearfoot.

Cheering on such research and development were a granddaughter and grandson of the company founder. They got into the fledgling stock outboard racing hobby and served as test drivers for the project. Two distinct high-speed lower units were tried on the Class

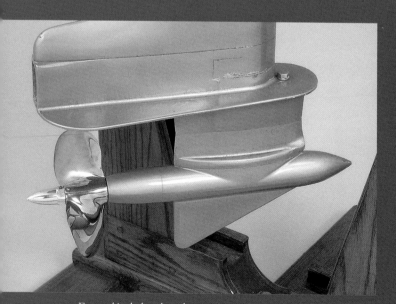

Even a bit sleeker than the competing Mercury Quicksilver racing gearfoot, is Chris-Craft's version.

"B" (20-cube) Commanders. The first, called an Algonac version (for the Michigan site where it was made) looked like the Merc Quickie foot from a distance, but differed inside. And, the Grand Rapids edition racing lower unit with a longer gearcase can be noted on our photographed motor. Only a handful of each racer was made by late 1952. The Grand Rapid's version was especially fast and could really give the similarly sized KG7Q or KG7H Quicksilver stock racing outboards a run for its money. Chris-Craft envisioned great things for 1953. A 25-horse shift model was in the planning stages, and improvements like a newly contoured intake manifold were added to the Commander 10 for even greater zing at the "fast" setting. It isn't far-fetched to imagine Chris-Craft outboards hitting the market's critical mass circa 1954 with the 5 1/2, the 10, and proposed 25 repositioned on family-friendly shift lower units. Then, there'd be a specialty line of these powerheads on racing lower units. A full line with such renown would have been in a position to surpass Mercury sales.

Someone brought to E. Carl Kiekhaefer's attention the fact that at least five features on the Commander were provinces of Mercury patents. No one has ever supposed that the similarities were the intentions of Chris-Craft officials. In fact, when threatened by Mercury with legal action, the boat company decided to end outboard production in 1953. Two years later, the designs (plus shifter lower units) appeared as Oliver branded products. The famous tractor maker had acquired Chris-Craft's quickly closed outboard motor facility, but never overtly pursued stock racing. Engines like our photographed subject piece are all that is left of a true blue contender.

Here are two examples of mid-50s Chris-Craft dealer signs.

"Today's Most Powerful Outboard!"

MERCURY MARK 50E

Brand Name: Mercury
Model: Mark 50E "Thunderbolt MercElectric"
Serial Number: 790879
Year of Manufacture: 1954
Manufacturer: The Kiekhaefer Corporation
Place of Manufacture: Fond du Lac, Wisconsin
Type: Two-cycle, Water-cooled
Number of Cylinders: 4
Bore X Stroke: 2-7/16" X 2-1/8"
HP @ RPM: 40 @ 5400
Weight: 120 lbs.
Original Price: $789.95
Owner: Robert Grubb

Blame it on the odd batch of Pyramid 3 parts that E. Carl Kiekhaefer found in the defunct Thor factory. Or maybe it was just his quantitative mindset that started the fledgling outboard maker thinking up ways to beat the competition using a tall row of cylinders. Whatever his intrinsic motivation, the Merc chief was happy to introduce motors with more pistons generating more horses than those of his rivals. In 1957, Kiekhaefer's top model boasted three times the cylinders and nearly double the power of anything Evinrude or Johnson offered. Admittedly, this 60-plus hp, six-in-line, Mark 75 was not actually his idea, but when Merc exec Charles Strang authorized a prototype, Kiekhaefer took it for a short ride and returned to the dock with the terse directive, "It speaks with authority. Build it!"

Some view Mark 75 as the first big, modern Mercury; thus the mill that spawned today's huge, full-featured, electro-mechanical outboards. Arguably, though, the obscure Mark 50 of 1954 set such a pace. Largely unsung by the very next boating season, this single-year motor ushered in an age of Mercury's chrome wrap-around shrouds, "Cowl-Around" carrying handle, electric starting, and assumption that the outboard would be remotely steered and controlled. The highly buffed, silver and cedar green machine also heralded Kiekhaefer's marketing paradigm shift away from high-strung, personalized racers and single-digit horsepower fishing engines to a new breed of thrust-laden family water-skiing motors.

Mark 50's ads usually included at least one picture of multiple or trick skiers, and emphasized the engine's brute force. "Fun?" its copy wondered, then con-

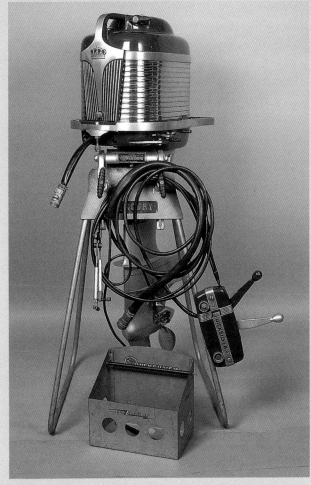

"The big Kahuna" for 1954 was Mercury's 40-horse Mark 50E with forward, neutral, and reverse. The "E" stood for electric starting and the motor is shown with its Quicksilver controls (some were labeled "Kaminc") with push-button choke and key in the ignition switch. The wiring harness and accessory, MercElectric 12-volt battery box is also shown.

firmed, "You know it when the power's by Mercury [Mark 50], the outboard that made water-skiing everybody's sport!" This statement co-opted considerable history from Evinrude and Johnson 25-horse motors, the full gearshift twins most responsible for making water-skiing a feasible, middle class, family activity. Merc officials realized the sport had a greater capacity to sell big (and profitable) motors than stock racing ever would, so used Mark 50 to

Move Up TO A

KIEKHAEFER

MERCURY

pick of the pilots and choice of
top-flight sportsmen everywhere

THE FINEST NAME
IN OUTBOARDS

CONSISTENTLY BETTER
ENGINEERING

Here is the Mercury KG-9 as presented on the cover of the 1952 brochure. this motor served as the basis for the in-line four Mark 50. Arguably, the KG-9, albeit underrated at 25 hp, could be faster than Mark 50, but its lack of a gearshift kept many buyers away.

begin breaking into that lucrative market. The company even had a booklet authored that it hoped would expedite a link to this new breed of outboard buyer. *How to Water Ski With An Outboard* could be had for the asking by mail or, better yet, at one's local Merc dealer where the motors in the pages were ideally on display.

Alas, the big Merc seemed in relatively short supply. Many small-town outboard fans only caught a glimpse of the Mark 50 in the aforementioned ads while more urban boaters might have spotted one between the early winter boat shows and the middle of the summer. But when a Mark 50-powered boat did happen by, folks on the shore knew it sounded more mature and exuded greater confidence than the usual OMC fare.

The Mark 50 traces its roots to the non-shift, 40-cubic inch KF-9, KG-9, and Mark 40. From 1949 through 1953, these four-in-line, rope-start "Thunderbolt" models were most popular with hot rodders and stock outboard racers, each unofficially conducting thousands of hours of in-field testing that confirmed the powerhead design's strengths and invited refining. Around 1948, there had been an opposed four-cylinder Thunderbolt in the works (using two sets of bow and stern-pointing KE7 Lightning blocks), but it never left prototype stage. Instead, stacking cylinders became Mercury's proclivity and chief franchise. Our featured motor contains another pioneering Kiekhaefer feature — a 12-volt electrical system with both a starter and generator. This option alone made the Mark 50 a runaway choice for outboard cruiser owners. Competitors' six-volt, "start-only" systems came up short (sometimes making for stone-dead batteries) in comparison.

Forty horsepower represented rarified outboarding air in 1954. Martin had hoped to put its 40-horse prototype into production, but the brand died on the vine that year. Power-wise, Mercury clearly stepped out in front. One can imagine the photographed outboard having been proudly selected to bond with a sturdy family runabout or small cruiser filled with picnic cooler, orange

life jackets, several towels, a little flag, one of those little over-the-side ladders, and brightly-colored water skis. The ignition key, affixed to a tiny buoy embossed with the dealer's name, would be part of Dad's domain, but the kids might beg for a chance to start the big Merc via a twist of the wrist. And who could have resisted easing the throaty-purring motor forward by nudging a lever on the remote controls, then letting the other lever tell all four pistons and the crankshaft they were free to play in the 5000 RPM range. If Norman Rockwell had been commissioned to paint 1954 Mercury calendars, he might have given the motor a big family to dote over its friendly power and beauty. In fact, the artistic promotional rendering of Mark 50 showed identification logos on the front and sides that never appeared on production motors. And that may be the secret of the Mark 50's elegance. There's something about the lone red crown emblem on the face plate that leaves one thinking such a motor truly requires no introduction.

big boat—
big load
outboard cruising's *all fun!*

with the incomparable
NEW **40** s.a.e. H.P.

KIEKHAEFER
MERCURY mark **50**

✳ Ball and Roller Bearings Throughout
$000.00

For sheer pleasure, there's nothing like an outboard cruise . . . and nothing like the mighty new Mark 50 for speed, super-smooth power and performance! Most compact outboard power plant ever built . . . with famous Thunderbolt engine, 4 cylinders in line, alternate firing . . . forward, neutral and reverse . . . new "Hi-Thrust" lower unit . . . power that handles big jobs with effortless ease . . . and famed Kiekhaefer Full Jeweled Power*!

See the 15th Anniversary Mercury Line at

DEALER NAME

MERCURY SUPER SILENT SIX

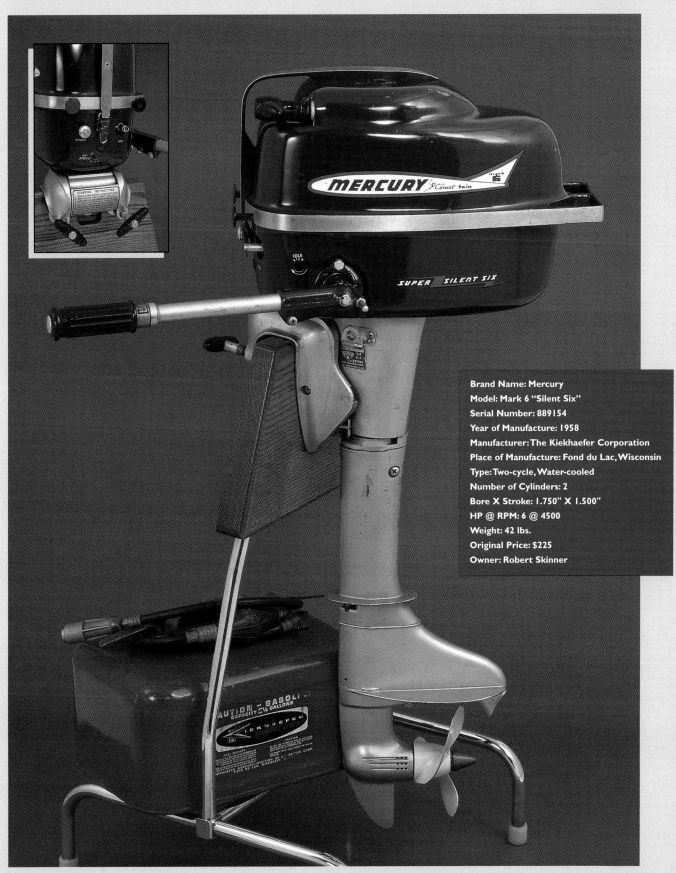

Brand Name: Mercury
Model: Mark 6 "Silent Six"
Serial Number: 889154
Year of Manufacture: 1958
Manufacturer: The Kiekhaefer Corporation
Place of Manufacture: Fond du Lac, Wisconsin
Type: Two-cycle, Water-cooled
Number of Cylinders: 2
Bore X Stroke: 1.750" X 1.500"
HP @ RPM: 6 @ 4500
Weight: 42 lbs.
Original Price: $225
Owner: Robert Skinner

Main picture: On some Mark 6 motors made after 1955, the I.D. tag said 5.9 hp rather than six. Some believe this had to do with horsepower limits on small lakes. Note: the fuel tank pictured has a 1960's-era decal.

Inset, top left: Press red for neutral and black for forward — the little plastic buttons on Mark Six took care of such direction, and a twist grip tiller worked the steering and throttle.

The old fisherman felt a bit odd standing quietly in front of Mercury's factory, but when the photographer ordered, "Smile," he did try. Little more than a grimace got on film. Posing next to him was E. Carl Kiekhaefer. He looked a bit happier having been reunited with a 1939 Thor-based outboard said to be the first one built by the then nascent Kiekhaefer Corporation. In exchange for that old motor and photo opportunity, the angler took home a new 1957 Mercury Mark 6 or "Silent Six." It wasn't a bad swap for the fisherman, and it was certainly worthy of a bigger grin, for he'd just acquired a motor known for its outstanding reliability.

In fact, Kiekhaefer — for PR purposes — had just given up one of Merc's best sellers for a real clunker. The old Thor and the new Mark 6 were as different as day and night, and the Mark 6 embodied the many Mercury innovations advanced in just under two busy decades. While a Thor owner might have brought up the fact that his motor ran well enough to chance a several mile putt-putt to some secret fishing spot, the Mark 6's performance would seldom give its owner cause for worry.

The Mark 6 was, in fact, the newest "little" Mercury. A 5 1/2-cubic-inch single had preceded it. That motor, known as the "Comet," was offered in denominations ranging from 3.1 to 3.6 horsepower from war's end through 1950. The year before being dropped, it was joined by the Super 5 (model KF5), later called Mark 5. Both of these five-horse motors

POWERFUL YET LIGHTWEIGHT

MERCURY

only
42 pounds ... packed with **BIG** features!

6 h.p.
Up to
24 months
to pay

MERCURY MARK 6

Here's the *big* buy in small motors! Enjoy Mercury's Push-Button Drive and convenient Twist-Grip Throttle. Forget about shear pins . . . dependable safety clutch eliminates them! Pull the handle and the Mark 6 tilts into weedless position! Anti-friction bearings . . . many other features. See them all today!

AS LOW AS **$00** DOWN

DEALER IMPRINT

were based on the 7.2 cubic inch block that would serve as the basis for the Mark 6. The latter, however, would have a bigger carb and produce higher RPM. Officially dubbed the Mark Six, it was also referred to variously as the "Silent Six," "Super Silent Six," and, harking back to the earlier littlest Mercs, "the Comet."

Our subject motor was found during the mid-1990s at Bluffton, Ohio, and survives in excellent original condition. The lucky collector who spotted it reports that his purchase "starts and runs very nice." When it left the factory in 1958, the Mark 6 probably went to a Midwestern dealer adept at explaining why one should pay a bit more for Merc's entry-level six-hp outboard as opposed to a three horse from Johnson or Evinrude. Of course, then he would be in a position to recommend a slightly larger boat, too. That wise old proprietor might suggest that, as they got used to their rig, new boaters tended to quickly tire of a three, but would probably be quite satisfied with the Mark 6.

During Mark 6's 1955-1959 run (the last year as Mark 6A), a fair number of small boat makers featured the model in their advertising. Performance with a Mark 6 was far snappier than that of OMC's small engines, and much more agile than what one could get out of the growing list of second-string, small-horse-power, bargain outboards like Clinton or Continental. Aluminum boat manufacturer Duratech understood that speediness could even entice low-end consumers. Consequently, during several boating seasons, the Pleasantville, New York company tested its small hulls with Mark 6 power, and suggested 18 to 20-miles per hour was attainable. That's going right along for a 10-foot fishing boat and approximately six-horse motor. Of course, not everyone cared to attempt local cottage racing records. In that case, Mark 6 was happy trolling, or even idling in neutral. The model consisted of spry little mills that looked to be happy to be working.

For some reason, our particular outboard's original purchaser put but a few hours on it in the nearly 40 years that he owned the rich green and silver motor. Perhaps he'd smile to have known that such a gentle schedule would someday net it a prominent picture in a book. Meanwhile, the buff who now has the little Merc, finds the "Super Silent Six" designation on the cowl to be somewhat odd. For something that's supposed to be "Super Silent," he admits, "this motor sure makes enough noise!"

Look! *Your Lipstick Matches Our Motor!*

JOHNSON JAVELIN

Brand Name: Johnson
Model: RJE-18 "Javelin"
Serial Number: 1369140
Year of Manufacture: 1956
Manufacturer: Johnson Motors
Place of Manufacture: Waukegan, Illinois
Type: Two-cycle, Water-cooled
Number of Cylinders: 2
Bore X Stroke: 2-7/8" X 2-3/4"
HP @ RPM: 30 @ 4000
Weight: 128 lbs.
Original Price: $582
Owner: Arthur DeKalb

On July 4th, 1956, an ad appeared in the Syracuse *Post-Standard* newspaper inviting Central New Yorkers to take a peek at a new housing development called Bayberry. Like the grand openings of many other such "planned communities" throughout North America, the Bayberry debut attracted thousands of 30-somethings who were looking for a little place of their own in the suburbs. It took only 18 minutes for the first house there to be sold. And, all of the other lots in Bayberry's initial section were taken by that afternoon. Instant suburbia promised young families a way to define themselves. While most of the five-room, $14,000 to $19,000 houses were essentially the same, adept 1950s suburban couples quickly learned how to play the game of transforming their little boxes into unique homes. Typically, this was done using little more than a tone or two of bold color and some inexpensive landscaping accents. Outboard makers knew of this trend. They schemed busily to have their motors be pretty enough to accent the bright new 15-foot family runabouts kept on shiny yellow trailers in the hot black macadam driveways. It was all a part of post war's good life package. Followers embraced the mantra; "Plain-Jane" was out. "Sporty" was in.

Outboard "motor designs for 1956 emphasize style" admitted boating columnist Hank Wieand Bowman, "[but offer only] modest mechanical improvements [over last year]." In *Boat Show*, a fun, pulpy, greenish half-tone photo-filled magazine cataloging the 1956 pleasure boating scene, he devoted considerably copy to Johnson's new look. Gone was the decade-long Sea Horse tradition of "sea mist green." To entice sporty outboard buyers — many of whom now included a female — the Johnson line was reinvented via "a metallic bronze finish which reflects and, chameleon-like, seems to adopt the color of any hull to which the motor is applied." And, for the first time since 1929, a Sea Horse was not Queen of the Johnson line. Instead, the new monarch wore the name Javelin in sporty script that gave the "J" a motion not possible with less imaginatively styled lettering. Of course, five horses had just been added to the bigger Johnsons' output, but with Mercury still leading the power race by a cool 10-hp margin, Johnson sleight of hand reached for the paint and trim. "The customized leader of the '56 Johnson

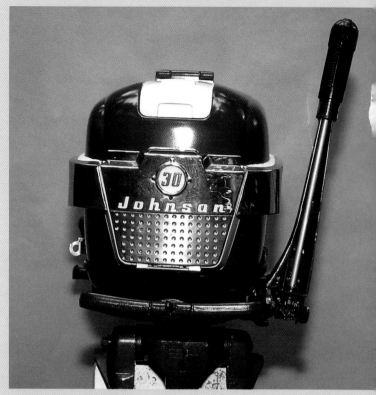

This was the color scheme that Johnson felt would match any 1956 boat — metallic bronze, bright white, and chrome. The tiller handle is an unusual Javelin accessory, as most were simply fitted with a metallic bronze painted linkage gear stub cover and black emergency speed control lever.

Here's what a Javelin looks like when she's not wearing makeup or, in this case, when her pull cord cover is removed and carburetor control door is down. Some Javelin "slow speed/high speed" faceplates were done in black.

line," Bowman confirmed, "is the Javelin, trimmed in bronze, white, and stainless steel." While accentuating essentially the same powerhead of OMC 25s from five years earlier, the stainless steel trim defined the motor. A dance of reflections in Javelin's chromed front panel no doubt added to countless summer memories. With eyes closed, the author vividly recalls a shimmery image of his Dad at the wheel of the family Lone Star runabout and the way that his kid sister's smiley, freckled face seemed to form around the little compass-like emblem that stated this motor was a 30.

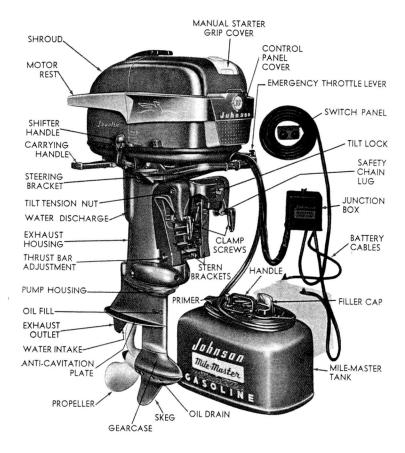

Like the creative suburban homeowners who admired the Javelin, Johnson augmented its resources through considering trim differences palpable enough to create new identity. This allowed Johnson to offer the Javelin 30 (which had six-volt electric starting), and the exact same motor, but without the trim (Sea Horse 30 Electric), as well as Plain Jane (Sea Horse 30) version that had to be pull-cord started. About $120 separated the ends of this 30-horse Johnson spectrum for 1956, significant green in that $80 per-week world. Still, the Javelin was such a profitable product that Johnson trimmed its 1958 version (by then 35-hp) in gold.

Paint played a major role in our subject Javelin, as its various owners have re-sprayed it several times. In their showrooms, savvy dealers often touted a small point-of-purchase display rack stocked with cans of their brand's "official" colors. Touch-ups were recommended as part of a motor's winter storage regimen. Of course, while fresh and shiny, not every batch was a perfect match. This resulted in nuances of hues quite acceptable to average owners, but a "little off" in the minds of purists. Also a bit unique to our Javelin is its

tiller handle. Unless special-ordered, none were factory-equipped on Johnson's top-of-the-line model. It was assumed that remote throttle/shift control and wheel steering would be the right of every Javelin. The pictured tiller arm was purchased as an accessory, then dealer installed for a customer who might have been just superstitious enough to believe his modern marvel of industrial design would go mechanically pale and require up-close triage. Anyway, the auxiliary piece looks rather nice in a positive, upward position. There, on a color-coordinated new boat and trailer in the freshly paved driveway, its black plastic grip can salute suburbanites who enjoy noticing something a little bit unique in their neighborhood.

Can I Get That in Sarasota Blue or Sunset Orange?

MERCURY MARK 25

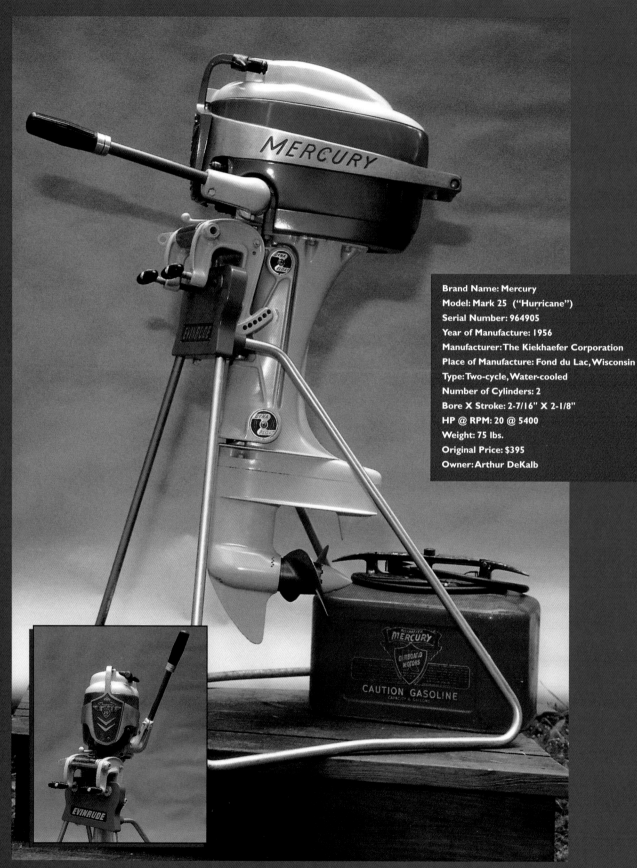

Brand Name: Mercury
Model: Mark 25 ("Hurricane")
Serial Number: 964905
Year of Manufacture: 1956
Manufacturer: The Kiekhaefer Corporation
Place of Manufacture: Fond du Lac, Wisconsin
Type: Two-cycle, Water-cooled
Number of Cylinders: 2
Bore X Stroke: 2-7/16" X 2-1/8"
HP @ RPM: 20 @ 5400
Weight: 75 lbs.
Original Price: $395
Owner: Arthur DeKalb

Merc's CEO could never be described as an old softie. He even fired a fellow for wasting time around the soda machine only to learn the man worked for a local bottler. But despite his black or white temper, E. Carl Kiekhaefer liked colors, and wanted lots of them to be designed into his outboards. A full model year before Evinrude or Johnson began stepping aboard the motor beautification bandwagon; Mercury's 1955 customers were granted several two-tone options on the newly introduced Mark 25.

In a way, the Martin people were responsible for Mark 25. Their introduction of the fast Martin "200" signaled Merc engineers that the KG7Q/KG7H and Mark 20 Hurricane series needed updating. Initially, this came in the form of the 1954 Mark 20H, which was actually a pre-production version of Mark 25. By the time the Mark 25 arrived on the scene, ironically, Martin was out of business.

The colorful new outboard was a hit with the boating press, which observed that such choice of colors was "met with enthusiastic response." Kiekhaefer responded by adding even more color schemes for 1956. Motors painted in any of four different two-toned paint schemes, or a newly mixed metallic green arrived at dealer showrooms in the fall of 1955 "so that buyers [could] match his [most probably his and her] motor to practically any boat's décor." Among the selection of "Merchromatic" colors were tan, Mercury green, a salmon hue, silver, a sand shade, sunset orange, and a palate of blues bearing image-dipped names like Sarasota, Marlin, Bimini, and Gulf. One of the least common combos on that option list, yet arguably its most peaceful, are the twin blue tones of our subject motor.

To be quite accurate, the Mark 25 for 1956 was not a sissy in any of the available garb. Upgraded from the previous year's debut, 18-horse Mark 25, the '56 (through 1958) version sported some 20 horsepower.

The block was based on the old KE7 Lightning's 20-cubic-inch cylinder arrangement, and also benefited from similarly sized KF7, KG7, Mark 20, and Mark 20H racer's high-revving technology.

Especially during the model's second generation (1956-1958), its soothing color schemes and non-threatening stature misled many outboard shoppers. But, the Mark 25's size could be especially deceptive to novices assuming it appropriate for a 12-foot aluminum rowboat. After all, the nicely presented Mercury weighed little more than an Evinrude or Johnson 10, and looked to be about the dimensions of a seven-and-a-half. One glance at the aggressive two-blade propeller Mark 25 could adroitly swing, however, should be clue enough that craft acceptable for other brands' motors of comparable physical dimensions, could prove dangerous with Mark 25 power. If light enough to allow the compact Merc's rated 5400 RPM to materialize, a boat and driver were in for quite a wild ride! Such performance would greatly diminish, though, with added cargo holding down the revs. Seeing a new Mark 25 forced to lug a trio of portly fishermen, their assorted gear, and a bulky fiberglass hull, an envious young outboarder sighed, "That's like buying a screen door for a submarine!"

Down on the motor leg, Mark 25 was fitted with two pairs of "Dyna-Float" suspension. The rubbery mounting points were designed to "isolate engine vibration from the boat and ease stress on the transom." Here, too, the little metal discs that covered these mounts were color-coordinated with one's overall paint scheme choice. Such attention to visual detail impressed even those who'd never been boating. Voting members of the Fashion Academy studied pictures of Mercs like our Mark 25 photograph. Balloting resulted in E. Carl Kiekhaefer winning the style organization's 1956 Gold Medal Award. A ribbon of red, white, and blue trimmed the honor's golden medallion. Merc's old man didn't really say much about recognition from the fashion sector, but quietly had a rendering of the medal included in his summer of '56 outboard advertising.

Detail opposite: This small package produces an honest 20-hp, but looks like competitors' 7 1/2-hp models! The two chevrons on Mark 25's faceplate indicate it's a 20-cubic inch engine. The 30-cube Mark 30 has three, and the 40-cubic inch piston displacement of Mark 55 has four such symbols on its front cover. The shift lever on this motor is right under the fuel connector for the remote tank. The little holes in the light blue casting near the bottom of the tiller and close to the shift are for a remote steering and shift/throttle control yoke. E. Carl Kiekhaefer would have fired the author (or at least throttled him) if he'd seen this motor on an official Evinrude stand!

WIZARD 25 AND MERCURY MARK 30H

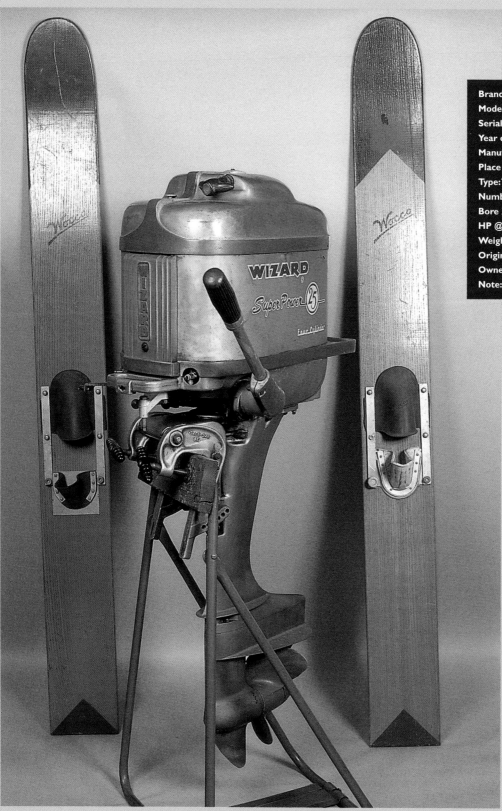

Brand Name: Wizard
Model: WA-25
Serial Number: 1016708
Year of Manufacture: 1957
Manufacturer: The Kiekhaefer Corporation
Place of Manufacture: Fond du Lac, Wisconsin
Type: Two-cycle, Water-cooled
Number of Cylinders: 4
Bore X Stroke: 2-7/64" X 2-1/8"
HP @ RPM: 25 @ 5000
Weight: 110 lbs.
Original Price: $399.50
Owner: Robert Grubb
Note: Sold through Western Auto Stores

The mid-1950s communiqué from a Western Auto Stores executive must have sparked at least a momentary flashback for E. Carl Kiekhaefer. It's quite possible that the call reminded the Merc chief about a similar request in 1940. Then, too, Western Auto wanted a completely new outboard design to sell and they had faith enough in Kiekhaefer's company to believe it could get the job done. Western Auto's connection with the Kiekhaefer Corporation had not only provided essential contracts and cash to Mercury, but gave the catalog store a line of outboards that, through the late 1950s, were considered by savvy boaters to be diamonds in the rough. That's not to imply that Wizard motors ever needed smoothing, as they were beautifully styled indeed. But, in a marketplace where mail order outboards were not expected to possess much more than the industry's most generic properties, Wizards held an enviable reputation for fast, reliable performance. Now, Western Auto requested a "big, green, waterskiing kind of Wizard"… and they wanted four cylinders.

It was the allure of the beautiful Mark 50 and the very notable sales success of Merc's colorful 1955 Mark 55 (successor to Mark 50) that gave Western Auto the idea for a comparable capstone outboard for its catalog and legion of shops. Kiekhaefer confidant Charles Strang had a head start on Western Auto. He'd already been considering building an in-line quad of just under 30-cubic inches for introduction into the starving Class "C" stock outboard racing sector. The Western Auto commission simply caused Strang to rally his troops for the making of a 30-cube Wizard prototype using two sets of pistons from Merc's 15-cubic inch engine. The dual-carbureted, in-line-four cylinder materialized in record time and Western auto got it in their brochures for 1956. Dubbed the Wizard "Super Power 25," some 15,000 were sold during a two-year run. That's a good number for a large-size private brand outboard, as most buyers of big engines had a penchant for entrusting their considerable investment only to one of the "major labels."

The poor man's big Merc, a Wizard 25 exhibits obvious Mercury traits such as cylinder arrangement, contoured tiller handle, barrel thumb screws, "arrow" starter pull, and basic cowl/handle design. Like other Merc Fours, it wears twin Tillotson carbs under the hood.

Word had spread, though, that Wizards were actually thinly disguised Mercs. That rumor was never too difficult to track down and verify. Wizard's 1955 brochure was full of clues. The twist grip speed control was identical to that depicted in Merc literature. Plus, any buff with a sharp eye noticed the two Mercury Mark 20 outboards — not Wizards — speedily pushing the cruiser on Wizard's catalog cover! Practically the only people who complained about this close association were Merc dealers who hated to see potential customers pick up a similar motor — for less money than one would pay for a genuine but comparable Mercury — at the local Western Auto.

Our photographed Wizard looks little different than it did when new, during the summer of 1957. No doubt a few scratches and some sun fade took place that season, but never marred the slow-troll-to-high RPM that a big, versatile, family outboard should offer. It was light enough for Dad to lift onto the boat with just a bit of help. The steering handle, with twist speed control, made for as convenient operation as did the shift lever peeking under the lower front cowl. Of course, an optional set of Kaminc (thinly masking the identity of another Merc-related division, Kiekhaefer AeroMarine, Inc.) remote controls would really complete the package. An electric start version (WAE-25) of the big green Wizard was also available. Whatever the configuration, the Wizard could offer a budget minded family a nice range of fun on the water — from fishing and cruising, to cottage racing and skiing.

Even before the first Wizard 25 was shipped, Charlie Strang knew Merc dealers would be clamoring for one like it, but different. While the four-cylinder Wizard technically came first, Mercury's 30-cube version followed closely enough to also be cataloged as the Mark 30 for 1956. This might be considered backwards protocol because catalog motors like Western Auto's were typically slightly outdated versions of their related "mother outboards." To balance the equation and keep Merc dealers from going ballistic, Strang made sure the Mark 30 was finely tuned to yield 30 horses instead of Wizard's 25. Concurrent with the new motors' arrival was the debut of the sportiest of that trio, the Mark 30H. Like the Wizard, the "regular" Mark 30 found quick acceptance in the lucrative pleasure boating milieu. Ads noted that it was "the motor you asked for," tying into a highly rated TV show of the period, *You Asked For It!* Upfront, Merc ads admitted that this all-around outboard weighed 110 pounds but stressed the inclusion of front and back carrying handles that "actually make it seem lighter." A 12-volt electric starter and generator could be ordered for more permanent installations.

Meanwhile, buyers for the Mark 30H stock racer, like the motor pictured here, quickly lined up. They were mostly stock outboarders who wanted to try enlivening the erstwhile moribund "C" Class. Since about 1945, it had been the province of a few diehard 30-cubers with gas/oil-fired (as opposed to alcohol based fuels) pre-war Evinrude and Johnson opposed twins that took racing runabouts into the low 40 mph range. The 30H immediately made this a contest of apples and oranges, as a representative example could zip a "C" Stock hydro past the mile-a-minute mark. Lots of this added speed came from the 30H Quicksilver lower unit.

By 1956, racers understood the benefits of running shallow — or surfacing — propellers where tremendous hydrodynamic advantage is gained by having very little of the lower unit, and only one prop blade at a time, in the water. That's why the 30H skeg is long and the cooling water inlet is on the underside of the 1:1 ratio gearcase. All Mark 30 models had a singularly cast cylinder block to facilitate improved cooling water jacket area. This fought heat-induced metal distortion in the cylinders and over the pistons, a battle weapon the racers especially appreciate. Besides the "Quickie" lower unit, peculiar to the 30H was a four-inch diameter (compared to the standard motor's eight) flywheel. In racing, lightness counts.

Figures show that less than 2,500 of the 30H models were produced. Most (about 2,100) came off the line in a 1956 and then a 1958 run. Another small batch was whipped up in 1959 as an uncataloged special for some dealers with stock racing ties. For the sake of musing, buffs often count the 30H as the last true factory racer from the great Merc/stock outboarding era of the boating boom 1950s. Added to such discussion is usually a story about how some of the leftover 1958 Mark 30 competition motors were taken from their "Quickies" and bolted to regular lower units, then shipped to interested dealers as standard Mark 30 discount models. Devotees might imagine a former 30H, never having had a chance to race, being reassigned to fishing motor duty. One buff believes he's found such a Merc. "Every time I take that pretty Sunset Orange and White beauty anywhere near a speeding boat," he smiles, "somehow it seems like the old gal moves the tiller in that direction. I guess she still hears the call."

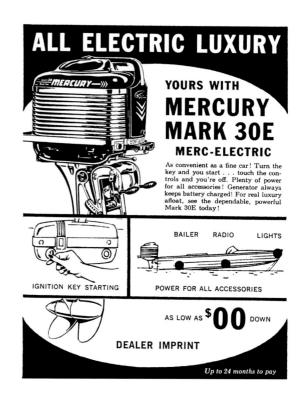

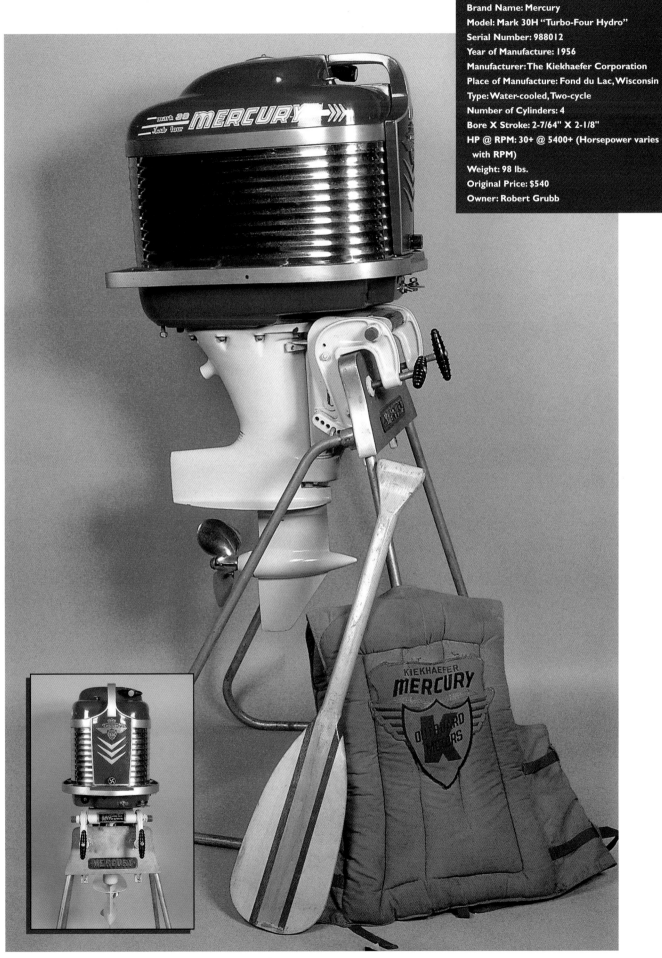

Brand Name: Mercury
Model: Mark 30H "Turbo-Four Hydro"
Serial Number: 988012
Year of Manufacture: 1956
Manufacturer: The Kiekhaefer Corporation
Place of Manufacture: Fond du Lac, Wisconsin
Type: Water-cooled, Two-cycle
Number of Cylinders: 4
Bore X Stroke: 2-7/64" X 2-1/8"
HP @ RPM: 30+ @ 5400+ (Horsepower varies with RPM)
Weight: 98 lbs.
Original Price: $540
Owner: Robert Grubb

Detail: The Hydro-Short "H" length Quickie lower unit — water pick-up on the gearcase's underside and long skeg — allowed 30H racers to run with water just covering the gearcase. This reduced drag enough to add several mph to a number of previous 30-cubic inch class "C" speed records. The ignition kill switch on lower "belly pan" cowl is a safety precaution.

The Brand X File Motor

CONTINENTAL SPORT

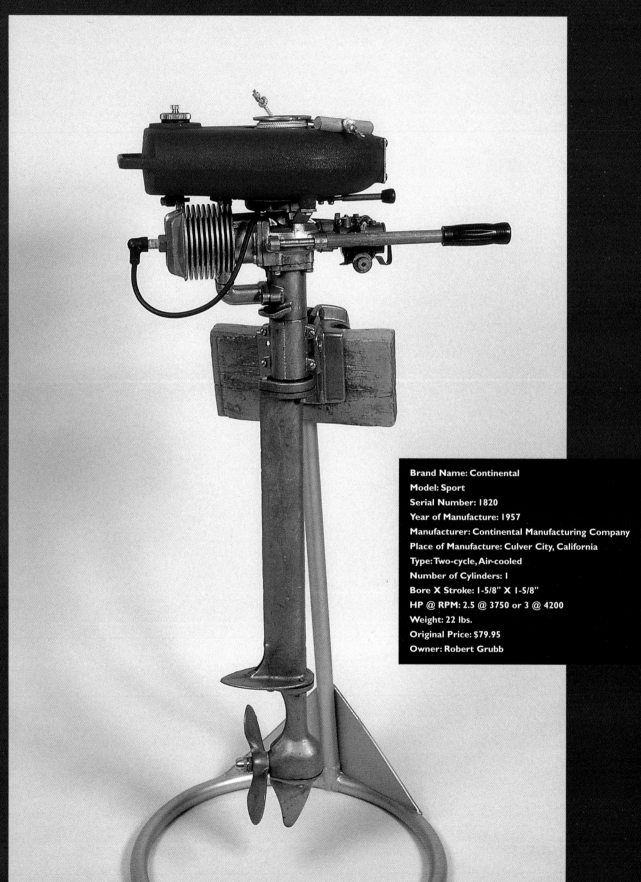

Brand Name: Continental
Model: Sport
Serial Number: 1820
Year of Manufacture: 1957
Manufacturer: Continental Manufacturing Company
Place of Manufacture: Culver City, California
Type: Two-cycle, Air-cooled
Number of Cylinders: 1
Bore X Stroke: 1-5/8" X 1-5/8"
HP @ RPM: 2.5 @ 3750 or 3 @ 4200
Weight: 22 lbs.
Original Price: $79.95
Owner: Robert Grubb

"I'd have a better chance sighting Elvis at my local convenience store," a vintage outboard buff admitted. In the late 1990s, he conducted a fruitless search for clues about a bargain-basement kicker with a long but seemingly vanished past. From the autumn of 1948 through the 1970s, a cheap outboard — often described as a Milburn Cub-type — made its way from pillar to post in Southern California before all traces of its origin went cold shortly thereafter. That's not to say none of these motors exist. Dozens are in the hands of collectors, and additional examples, sometimes with heretofore unknown branding, pop up on a surprisingly regular basis. Quite odd, however, is the fact that nobody, not even current owners of the various Los Angeles area buildings where the engines were assembled, has any idea of their predecessor's whereabouts or even a scintilla of detail concerning such motors. It all makes for a rather mysterious story.

Around Christmas 1948, tiny ads for "the world's lowest priced precision outboard motor" appeared in a few publications like *Popular Science*. As one might expect from such publicity, they were filled with hyperbole about easy starting, consistent slow trolling, responsive speeds up to eight miles-per-hour, safety gas tank (whatever that meant?), and a motor with "all wanted features." Of course "valuable territories" just happened to still be open to dealers and distributors.

The 2 1/2-horse mill had rope start and underwater exhaust via a long tube from the cylinder. By adding $3 to the introductory $69.50 price, one could have the old-fashioned exhaust tube replaced with a small casting that diverted fumes down the driveshaft housing. Dubbed the "Cub," these motors were offered by the H.B. Milburn Company of 11861 South Main Street in Los Angeles. Sometime in 1950 or 1951, they were being handled by L.K. Products of nearby Culver City. It's unclear how long that lasted, as virtually no "Cub" advertising exists from the 1951-1955 period. Cub-like outboards (not to be confused with the 1939-1942 Elto Cub) wearing Water Masters Incorporated, Bud Bilt Manufacturing Company, or Wego Motor Company (all Los Angeles) tags probably hail from this era. They may well be a trail of micro-manufacturers that each took a brief shot in the outboard game.

Here's what a 1957 Continental "Sport" looks like straight out of the shipping carton. It was found as "new old stock" in a defunct dealer's estate. Scratches and paint nicks are pretty much standard issue for these bargain-built outboards. Note the simple choke butterfly mechanism, lack of protection over the Tillotson brand carburetor intake (OK in racing installations but not for fishing motors), and tiller handle on the "wrong" side or at least opposite the position of most every other brand's steering arm. The wooden starter handle and associated rope is reminiscent of some last minute Cub Scout project. It, too, is "factory stock" from the mysterious Continental headquarters.

Our photographed kicker is a product the Continental Manufacturing Company. This firm was headquartered at 10401 Washington Boulevard in Culver City, just a stone's throw from the old MGM movie studios. It appears they were keepers of the Milburn design from about 1956 to 1964. Continental dropped the "Cub" nomenclature in favor of "Sport, Commando, Deluxe," et al. While sundry pieces of the Continental's "Marine Division" (likely a designated corner of their shop) literature and motors have surfaced, its officials escaped without a trace. Small print in the 1959-1960 Culver City directory does turn up the names of two principals, but identifies them as makers of auto parts, not outboards. Whether the motors were actually produced there is unknown. It's possible that the parts were cast elsewhere, then assembled at Continental's modest HQ.

Ads boasted of skilled aircraft designers being responsible for the little motor "under the supervision of experienced engineers in a completely equipped modern machine plant." Of course if they were truly adept at their trade, they'd be busy designing planes rather than fooling with some blowout priced outboard. Actually, Continental got pretty good coverage of its early marine endeavors. The boating press was sure to note the then $79.95 motor in its exposes. Just the fact that the product could be bought for 40 percent less than a comparable Evinrude or Johnson earned it editorial space. And when Continental decided to offer the package in do-it-yourself form, even the January 1957 *Popular Mechanics* ran an article on the novel kicker kit. It was thought that one could not tell the difference between a kit and a factory assembled Continental. Turns out though, that the D-I-Y model was specifically branded "The Kit." Different from most competitors was Continental's removable powerhead. Flyers stated it could "be quickly removed and fitted to a special power takeoff mounting [so that] the engine [could be] used for either belt or direct drive to operate electric generators, pumps, saws. lawn mowers, and various kinds of machinery."

The photographed Continental represents the standard product of the tiny outboard enterprise. It and another Continental were found in unopened packing cartons in the remnants of a northern New England small engine shop. Fitted with a Tillotson carb instead of the primitive proprietary Milburn designed "bleeder" carburetion, our "Sport" exhibits the crude, rough aluminum castings quintessential to the marque.

There looked to be little in the way of quality control. Some motors came through smooth, while others really had the texture of a hurried high school project. Even the fuel tank is roughly sand cast with the motor nametag serving as a covering over the casting-core opening. This one is treated with red crinkle finish probably to mask imperfections. Others have been noted in a deeper flat red, brown, and bare aluminum. The integral handle cast into the end of the tank was prone to breakage. A machined aluminum pulley tops

the crankshaft. Continental also offered a Fairbanks-Morse rewind assembly, and an aftermarket electric starter (adapted to the Fairbanks-Morse unit) has also been seen. Besides the two different carbs, other variants include the double thumbscrew transom clamp as well as one with just a single tightener.

During the early 1960s, Continental Manufacturing Company shortened its name to Comanco, and began phasing out the old Milburn-type powerheads in favor of better running Tecumseh singles. Another firm, Ward International of Studio City, entered the mysterious picture with the "Husky," a Comanco-esque variation circa 1963 and 1965 through 1967. Also during this time, Commando Motors, 1583 Monrovia in Newport Beach, apparently acquired Comanco's (Continental) outboard interests and began marketing a line of low-priced motors. By the 1970s, these Tecumseh-powered kickers were being equipped with a newly designed lower unit — including a jet thrust variation — but faded from boating advertising within a few years. Investigation into this business was as equally unprofitable as attempts to locate Milburn and Continental parentage. Hence, the challenge is still active. This narrative is meant to show that part of the beauty of old outboards is found within the chase they inspire. Meanwhile, our subject Continental remains an enigmatic orphan.

The **MILBURN** *aircooled* **CUB**

A Bear for Power

at a Honey of a

price $**69**50

The Milburn Cub may have been the inspiration for the similarly priced Continental Sport.

ZÜNDAPP DELPHIN

Brand Name: Zündapp
Model: Delphin type 303
Serial Number: 506180
Year of Manufacture: 1960
Manufacturer: Zündapp Werke
Place of Manufacture: Munich, Germany
Type: Two-cycle, Air and Water-cooled
Number of Cylinders: 1
Bore X Stroke: 46 mm X 42 mm
HP @ RPM: 2.3 @ 4500
Weight: 29 lbs.
Original Price: US import price unknown
Owner: Robert Skinner

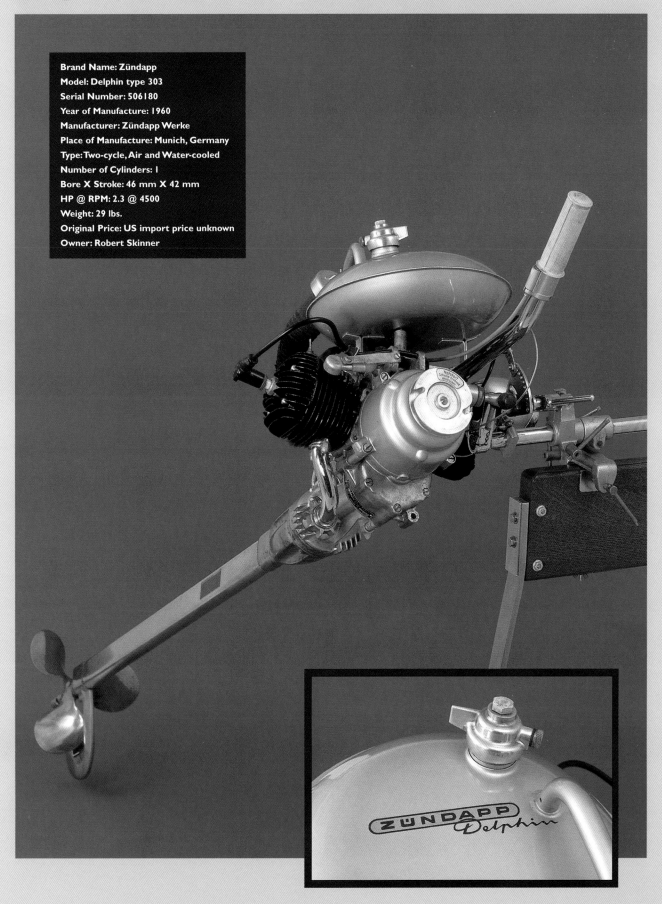

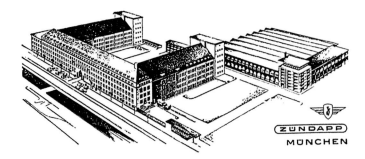

Long before Honda or Yamaha outboards began appearing on North American boats, a handful of imports paved the way for their invasion. Only British Sea Gull enjoyed even modest US and Canadian success prior to the1970s. For the eclectic motor buff, however, it was fun to spot the strange foreign brands that peeked into the outboard industry's tent during the first two decades after World War Two. One of the most unique was Zündapp's Delphin.

It appears that the earliest Zündapp kickers in America were 1955 offerings of the New York City-based Klepper Company, importers of the famous folding kayaks. Apparently Klepper imported them from the German firm and then private-branded the straight shaft outboards to bear the Klepper name. Most prominent on the three-horse @ 5000 RPM machine was a small adjustable searchlight affixed to the fuel tank. By 1960, Zündapp had it's own distributor in Connecticut to handle the Munich manufacturer's sewing machines, small motorcycles (from a 50cc "Combinette" moped to the 245cc "Trophy 5" road bike), and Delphin outboard. To be sure, the latter had features not found in many other kickers.

Zündapp brochures tout "the way of the cooling water and exhaust gas flow in[side] the mounting bracket tube and shaft casing. The flow of the exhaust gases is so conducted as to accelerate and, at the same time, warm up the cooling water. The exhaust gases are expelled from the shaft and underwater." A snorkel hose fed air into the waterproof carburetor. A "water separator" on the carb diverted moisture away from the fuel Intake, allowing the motor to withstand periodic dunkings without stalling. Foul-weather sailors might find this trait most attractive. And, then there's the Delphin's "mini showerhead." It took warmed-up water from the pump/exhaust gas symbiosis and sprayed it over the finned cylinder as well as on the watertight sparkplug and wire.

Zündapp offered several kinds of motor mounting. For plank decks (typically sailboats) a horizontal-mounting bracket clamped to a post protruding from Delphin's side. Four bolts on this bracket attached through holes one would drill in the boat. A vertical bracket facilitated bolting through the stern. Most recommended, however, was Zündapp's "universal gunwale mounting arrangement" that wore a vice-like bracket on each end of a long, horizontal pole attached to the powerhead's side. Clamping this device to canoe or rowboat gunwales allowed for running the motor over the craft's side.

While arguably quite logical to the European market, that German way of bolt mounting an outboard to a boat seemed far too aggressive and complex to Americans and Canadians used to simply tightening a couple of thumbscrews on the transom bracket. Therein existed the highest barriers to the Delphin's wider acceptance in outboarding's most lucrative market. At the time, Zündapp was simply seen as unconventional. It also begged the question of why anybody who'd recently won a world war should have to bother adapting to the ways of the vanquished side. As it turned out, of course, Volkswagen cars, not Zündapp outboards, would provide an answer to that query. Then the Hondas and Yamahas followed.

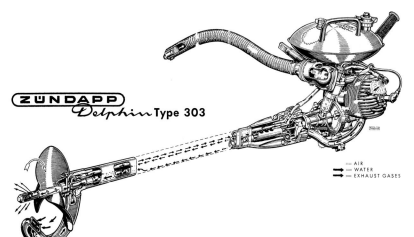

ZÜNDAPP
Delphin Type 303

= AIR
= WATER
= EXHAUST GASES

Theory Yes, Practice No

OUTBOARD JET

Brand Name: Outboard Jet
Model: OJ200
Serial Number: 10684A
Year of Manufacture: about 1967
Manufacturer: Outboard Jet, Incorporated
Place of Manufacture: Indianapolis, Indiana
Type: Two-cycle, Water-cooled
Number of Cylinders: 2
Bore X Stroke: 2-1/2" X 1-1/16"
HP @ RPM: 9.5 @ 4100
Weight: 62 lbs.
Original Price: $369.50
Owner: Robert Grubb

Water deflector nozzle

Water jet output

Water intake

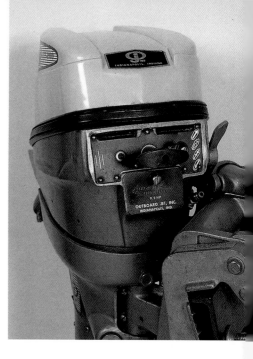

The model OJ200 instrument panel includes a choke knob, pull start handle, remote fuel line connector, and carburetor adjust cover. "Shift" symbolism instructions show water discharge's control lever position for (top to bottom) forward, trolling, neutral, and reverse. Throttle control is twist grip activated from the tiller.

A kid scoping out a vintage outboard from the dock laughed that it looked like a funny kind of jet-ski motor for rowboats. He thought about it for a while, then admitted that powering an ordinary fishing boat with water thrust wasn't such a bad idea. But the teenager's conclusion was linked to the hundreds of personal watercraft he'd seen skimming the lake. In 1967, observers of the Outboard Jet in action had no such paradigm reference. They could only compare it to "regular" outboard motors with real lower units and propellers. In that context, the thing seemed like a goofy contraption. Being ahead of one's time may yield eventual recognition, but retrospective offers little encouragement when the innovation is new. Such was the case with the model OJ200 Outboard Jet.

By the early 1960s, a number of so-called jet outboard motors had surfaced in the fishing motor milieu. Most were similar to Lancaster Pump's "Guppy," a basic underwater impeller pump powered by a simple lawnmower engine. These kickers, or more appropriately, "squirters," rotated water through their revolving door lower units to generate enough thrust for forward motion. Most hardly matched the stamina of the cheapest electric trolling motors. And. all sounded as loud and as industrial as a lawnmower going full blast.

Indianapolis-based Outboard Jet jumped into the genre with air-cooled Tecumseh powerheads, but rethought the discharge pattern to achieve good performance. The firm's initial offering reached the market in 1963, and featured a pumping system that shot output water from just about transom clamp level down to the lake or river surface. This worked much better than the likes of Guppy, encouraging officials of the fledgling Hoosier firm to spring for a proprietary powerhead powerful enough to generate some great publicity in the boating press.

The motor shown here is a fine, original example of Outboard Jet's most ambitious project. Beautifully crafted, the company's own 9 1/2-horse, loop-charged mill exhibited the quality of major outboard makers. Detailing is also as attractive as regular models from the big guys, with useful controls, sturdy die-casting, and attractive finish. The OJ200 even had a shift! Lever motion activated a hinged deflector at the water outlet "nozzle." With water shooting down vertical with the transom, a neutral is facilitated. Forward water deflection (towards the stern) is supposed to produce a reversing effect, but fails miserably on this motor. Forward motion (when water is discharged at about a 30-degree angle) is the Outboard Jet's strongest suit. Even so, the jet system doesn't seem to let those 9 1/2 horses act their size. The owner of this outboard estimates its performance might only rival that of the little TD-20, five-hp Johnson we featured in earlier pages of this book. Also disappointing was the tiller arm that only folds down and has no provision for keeping itself parallel to the operator's seat. Consequently, one has to hold it up as well as steer. Alas, it was probably the basic unconventionality of OJ200 that caused outboard shoppers to turn away. With 20-20 hindsight, though, one can see that its designers had a good idea; a concept that later would be replicated millions of times inside ubiquitous fleets of water-jet propelled personal watercraft.

Outboard Jet's generous water pick-up grates are prone to accumulate vegetation, thus truncating the outboard's performance in a milieu where water-thrust motors are supposed to excel — shallow, weedy lakes, ponds, and rivers.